HOW TO MAKE A HOME

ANCIENT WISDOM FOR MODERN READERS

■ ■ ■ ■ ■

HOW TO
MAKE A HOME

■ ■ ■ ■ ■ ■

An Ancient Guide to Style and Comfort

Vitruvius and Guests

Selected, translated, and introduced by
Marden Fitzpatrick Nichols

PRINCETON UNIVERSITY PRESS

PRINCETON AND OXFORD

Published by Princeton University Press
41 William Street, Princeton, New Jersey 08540
99 Banbury Road, Oxford OX2 6JX

press.princeton.edu

All Rights Reserved

ISBN 978-0-691-24912-4
ISBN (e-book) 978-0-691-27166-8

Library of Congress Control Number 2025935260

British Library Cataloging-in-Publication Data is available

Editorial: Rob Tempio and Chloe Coy
Production Editorial: Jill Harris
Text Design: Heather Hansen
Jacket Design: Heather Hansen
Production: Erin Suydam
Publicity: William Pagdatoon and Carmen Jimenez

Jacket image: Bronze statuette of a Lar. Courtesy of Rogers Fund,
1919 / The Metropolitan Museum of Art, New York

This book has been composed in Stempel Garamond and
Adobe Text with Futura

Printed in the United States of America

1 3 5 7 9 10 8 6 4 2

For my mother and father

"In the first place, parents are the builders
of their children."
—PLAUTUS, *Mostellaria* 120

CONTENTS

CONTENTS

ILLUSTRATIONS

PREFACE

Among the social changes attributable to the COVID-19 pandemic, which accelerated the spread of digital technologies across every domain of human experience, was an adjustment to the very definition of home. An uptick in remote work across many occupations in industrialized countries transformed "home" from a place of privacy, seen almost exclusively by family, friends, and invited acquaintances, to a backdrop for the performance of professional identity, transmitted via computer screen.[1] Meanwhile, as the impacts of the virus tethered people ever closer to their residences, buyers' increasing preference for larger houses drove up real estate prices, exacerbating disparities between rich and poor.[2] Demand for architects and contractors, home-improvement retailers, and purveyors of home furnishings likewise surged,[3] egged on by fantasies of renovation, DIY, and house-flipping that were already mainstays of social media and reality television.[4] Even as the specific contexts of the early 2020s recede into history, this flurry of interest in domestic space has left an indelible mark on the design of many residences and the ways in which they are used. Simply put, home matters like never before.

As we consider the ever-changing forms, styles, and meanings of our homes, there is wisdom and food for thought to be gained from an unexpected source: ancient Rome. The notion that residences played an essential role in creating and communicating professional identities was second nature to the Romans. Romans with the means to do so designed their homes to reflect not just a private self, shared with family and close friends, but also the image they wished to project to acquaintances and strangers, who visited the homes of the wealthy and powerful to transact business and maintain social, cultural, and political networks. "Working from home" was not a crisis accommodation, but integral to Roman architectural design.

The ancient Romans inhabited many different types of homes. They lived in huts and cottages, apartment buildings and townhouses, as well as residences on country estates located in the suburbs or countryside. A privileged few even lived in palaces. As is true in many societies today, owning a home (or devoting care to the decoration of a rental property) was a mark of privilege. Most people came home to very humble lodging, with little furniture and few belongings beyond some bedding and the most rudimentary utensils of daily life. Such modest forms of accommodation are occasionally imagined within the pages of this book. The reader will quickly discover, however, that townhouses and villas, and their owners, are its primary subject.

Two accidents of history have conspired to make evidence for townhouses and villas disproportionately available: the survival of a variety of texts (here surveyed across the period of the second century BCE to the second century CE) that elaborate on the forms and meanings of such structures, and the eruption of Vesuvius in 79 CE. The destruction wrought by the volcano paradoxically resulted in the preservation by burial of a substantial number of townhouses and villas along the Bay of Naples at the towns of Pompeii, Herculaneum, and beyond. This area of Italy, due to its land- and seascapes, favorable climate, mineral springs, and entertainment venues, was a destination for leisure and recreation in antiquity. The elite of Rome often summered on the Bay of Naples; vacation spots there appear frequently in Roman descriptions of a lifestyle of ease and pleasure associated with the villa as holiday home. Townhouses, meanwhile, lined the streets of urban centers, where most of the region's year-round population resided.

Just as the sites on the Bay of Naples form the nucleus of what is archaeologically known about ancient Roman townhouses and villas, the city of Ostia provides a treasury of evidence for ancient apartment living. Ostia was the port of Rome and the city's first colony. A major program of rebuilding in the second to early third centuries CE transformed the architectural face of Ostia, leaving behind brick-faced apartment blocks that can be visited today. Touring Ostia along with the Bay of Naples is an unparalleled way to appreciate Roman domestic architecture and design across two very different settings and periods.

There are many lavishly illustrated books (and websites) that offer non-specialist readers the opportunity to experience these spectacular ruins through photographs, digital models, and diagrams. This book has a different aim: to share a sampling of the most illuminating and thought-provoking ancient writings about Roman homes. In keeping with the established format of this book series, readerly imagination is favored over illustration. I hope that you will accept this invitation to enter Roman domestic space with ancient authors as your guides.

ACKNOWLEDGMENTS

The inspiration for *How to Make a Home* came from two previous authors of books in this series: I am grateful to Josiah Osgood, who envisioned an architectural volume and put my name forward, and to Johanna Hanink, who offered insights that shaped and guided the conception of the work from start to finish. Working with the indefatigable Rob Tempio and Chloe Coy at Princeton University Press, and with the generous comments of two anonymous readers for the Press, has been a privilege I do not take for granted. My continued enthusiasm for ancient Roman houses and villas is largely attributable to the pleasures of discussing this favorite topic with Hérica Valladares for many years. I owe a substantial debt of gratitude to Charles McNelis, who not only pored over the full manuscript and made crucial observations, but also animated the daily process of its creation with his generosity, discernment, and wit. Selections from the volume received valuable feedback from Mika Natif, Loxley Nichols, Rachael Nichols, Dylan Ryan, Carey Seal,

Alexander Sens, Katherine Wasdin, and Elizabeth Dospěl Williams. I am thankful above all to my husband and daughters, who are home to me.

This book is dedicated to two people whose passions and whose love provided its intellectual and practical foundation, my parents, Loxley and Andrew Nichols.

INTRODUCTION

William Morris (1834–1896) famously advised, "Have nothing in your house that you do not know to be useful, or believe to be beautiful." Morris spoke from a position of profound investment in the topic: as a textile designer, he was a leading voice in the Arts and Crafts Movement, which revitalized the decorative arts in Great Britain and beyond. Among ancient Roman thinkers, such sentiments circulated far beyond the realm of decorators, and indeed were considered vital to the flourishing of society as a whole. The scholar and author Marcus Terentius Varro (116–27 BCE), for example, claimed that usefulness (*utilitas*) and elegance of appearance (*elegantia*) were the two goals to be sought in the design of clothing, dishes, houses, and other objects of human creativity.[1] "We don't want to have a house," he explained, "just so that we can live under a roof and in a secure situation that necessity has corralled us into, but so that we can have a place where life's pleasures can be experienced."[2] The enthusiasm with which the Romans pursued this goal resulted in the wealth of perspectives offered by the authors included in this volume. On the subject of how to make a home, the Romans had much to say.

Two types of ancient Roman homes where the pursuit of elegance, beauty, and pleasure—the life of comfort and style—reached its zenith were the townhouse (*domus*) and the country estate residence, or villa (*uilla*). The former were built in cities and towns, and were the location *par excellence* of their owner's business interests (*negotium*). The latter could be found in suburban or rural settings and were imagined, at least, as places of pure pleasure and relaxation (*otium*). As these two types of residences will figure extensively in the ancient texts presented in *How to Make a Home*, a few words concerning their norms of configuration and decoration are warranted. Admittedly, it would be impossible to account for all the variation in the evidence for these structures: the survival of so many well-preserved townhouses and villas, particularly on the Bay of Naples, has enabled a more developed picture of ancient Roman domestic architecture and décor than is possible for almost any other pre-modern society in world history. As a result, every generalization offered here is just that. Exceptions attend every "rule." Nevertheless, when the authors surveyed in this volume invoked the townhouses and villas

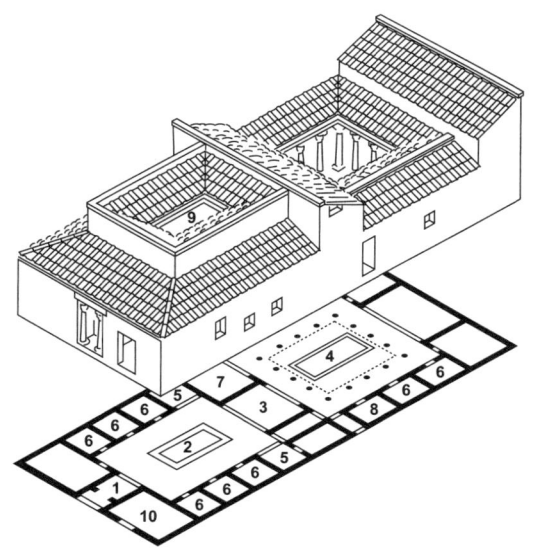

1. entrance (*fauces* and *uestibulum*)
2. *atrium* with *impluuium*
3. *tablinum*
4. *peristylium*
5. *alae*
6. *cubiculum*
7. *triclinium*
8. *culina*
9. *compluuium*
10. *taberna*

FIGURE I. Diagram of a Roman townhouse. Adapted from
E. La Rocca, M. de Vos, and A. de Vos, *Guida archeologica di
Pompei* (Milan: Mondadori, 1976).

of Roman Italy, they likely had the following broad expectations in mind.

Townhouse

Roman townhouses were designed to create oases of light and air, steps away from the commotion and noise of the street (fig. 1). Many townhouses were single-storied, and very few had more than two levels. Basements were rare. It was common for a townhouse to have one-room shops (*tabernae*), other businesses, or rental accommodations abutting its exterior, or in upper stories. The plaster facades of these houses were architecturally plain, though they could be adorned with spoils taken from the battlefield, including weapons and pieces of armor, a vivid reminder of the valorization of war and conquest in Roman society. As part of the urban streetscape, these facades might also be emblazoned with painted messages, some of which functioned as signage for political campaigns or local events. Exterior windows, which might be secured by bars or shutters, were few.[3]

The quintessential feature of the townhouse was a large open space called an *atrium*, adjoined by much smaller rooms along its periphery. Frequently, the *atrium* was exposed to the sky through a square opening (*compluuium*) in the roof. Vitruvius, author of *De architectura* (20s BCE), the only work dedicated to architecture that survives from Greek or Roman antiquity, records a typology of five types of *atria*, each distinguished by the pitch of its roof and the number of columns (if any) surrounding its *compluuium*.[4] Rainwater collected in a basin (*impluuium*) set into the floor, which might be connected to a cistern below. The *compluuium* also allowed smoke from the hearth or other fires to exit the house. The poet Juvenal (late first to early second century CE) thus refers to the portraits of the owner's ancestors, commonly located in the *atrium*, as "smoke-covered" (see passage 8). Just as these portraits established a link between the family's present and its past, so too did the presence of a small shrine to the household gods: alongside images of the deities who safeguarded the family and home (the *Lares* and *Penates*), there was often a painted or sculpted representation of the *genius*, the male spirit of the entire family or clan (*gens*), embodied by the head of the family (*paterfamilias*). The image of the *genius* was that of the *paterfamilias* himself in a toga, holding instruments of religious sacrifice. His head would be veiled in a display of piety.

The *atrium* was not only the religious core of the home, but also its social hub. As such, it often exhibited fine decoration, including brightly colored wall paintings and floor mosaics made of black and white (or, more infrequently, colored) stone cubes (*tesserae*). The *atrium* was the first room seen by entrants to the house. In many cases, it would have been visible from the street when the door was ajar. An open front door, staffed by an attendant, was itself a display of wealth. Thus, in the earliest surviving Roman novel, Petronius's *Satyrica*, the reader's initial glance into the enormous and extravagantly decorated townhouse of the affluent, if gauche, Trimalchio lands squarely on the sumptuously costumed person of the doorman.[5]

When not located directly behind the door, the *atrium* was reached via a narrow passageway (*fauces*), and perhaps a vestibule (*uestibulum*). Visitors welcomed into the home waited in the *atrium* for consultation with the *paterfamilias*. This might take place in the *tablinum*, an elegant room located at the far end of the *atrium*, which could be made more private through the use of curtains or doors. The frequency with which the doorway, *atrium*, *tablinum*, and beyond were laid out back-to-back, centered on an axis, suggests that such "axial alignment" was intentionally adopted as a means of creating a sightline deep into the house (see passage 4). The *paterfamilias* may well have taken advantage of this architectural means of centering attention when he acted as patron to a range of clients who came to visit him as part of a formal morning visit called the *salutatio*. The choreography of the *salutatio*, in which a powerful man remained at home, awaiting the obeisance of social inferiors, vividly illustrates the centrality of status hierarchies to Roman society (see passage 5). The impact of these hierarchies on the texts collected in this volume will quickly become apparent: while the family (*familia*) sheltered at a magnificent townhouse in the city or villa in the countryside often included an extended group of blood relations, as well as guests, boarders, and slaves, ancient authors amplify the perspectives of male homeowners, presenting a limited view of a context in which persons of disparate gender, class, and station lived and worked side by side.

Also located off the *atrium* were *cubicula*, small and often intimate spaces suitable as bedrooms, but flexible in function.[6] Lampooned in Petronius's *Satyrica* for his excessive spending and terrible taste, the aforementioned Trimalchio boasts that his home contains twenty *cubicula*.[7] This humorously inflated number exposes an underlying truth: whereas even an enormous townhouse would possess two *atria* at most, *cubicula* were commonly several in number. Given the modest scale of these rooms, some were used for storage or mundane daily activities.

Decoration was therefore crucial for establishing an elevated ambience. Floor mosaics and wall paintings (frescoes) conveyed these cues.

Roman floor mosaics were enlivened by complex geometric patterns, in seemingly endless variety. The finest mosaics were analogous to paintings, as they depicted landscapes and complex figural scenes. Over the course of the first century BCE, the painted designs on Roman walls evolved from a "masonry style," mimicking the appearance of marble cladding, to more complex compositions depicting columns and other architectural motifs. On the walls of some houses, scenes of landscapes and buildings almost tricked the eye with their realism. By the end of the first century BCE, imitations of panel paintings became integral to many designs, so that, at first glance, scenes of figures appear to be portable works of art, rather than elements of a fresco. Even in finely decorated homes, however, the surfaces of most walls were left as plain plaster or decorated with stripes or simple geometric schemes. Likewise, mosaic pavements were such a special expense that many floors were laid with concrete; scattered tiles or marble fragments would create a more finished look.

While wall paintings and floor mosaics were fixed in place, this was hardly true of most other furnishings. Roman furniture, made of wood, was light and moveable. This not only enabled individual rooms to be configured differently at short notice to accommodate changing activities, but also facilitated seasonal migration around the house by occupants eager to make use of a sunny spot in winter, or the breeziest chamber in the summer heat. Metal braziers were the most common form of temperature control, as under-floor heating fed by furnaces was largely limited to bath complexes. Depending on the time of year, dining might take place in different locations within the Roman townhouse. (Trimalchio alleges that he has four dining rooms, presumably one for each season.)[8]

The Latin word for a dining room (*triclinium*), derived from Greek, refers to the presence of three couches, placed at right angles, thus forming three sides of a rectangle. The designs of mosaic floors in *triclinia* sometimes include lines to indicate the customary locations of these couches. The open fourth side allowed the meal to be served, as well as made possible the enjoyment of theatrical, musical, and literary performances, the favored entertainments at dinner parties. Another popular activity, according to ancient authors, was intellectual debate or banter inspired by the works of art that decorated the home. In the dining room itself, focus would naturally land on the wall paintings, which frequently took up Greek mythological themes. Even objects of tableware, however, emblazoned with figural motifs, could inspire contemplation and conversation.

In the domestic architecture of our own time, an "open plan," achieved by tearing down walls between kitchens and dining rooms, betrays a desire for the activities of the kitchen to be incorporated into the living spaces, allowing conversation and other interactions across these areas of the house. This inclination presents a strong contrast with ancient Roman townhouses, where an openness of layout extending to the kitchen (*culina*) was undesired. Instead, walls confining the heat, smells, and smoke of the kitchen were favored. Likewise, while in many homes today, the appliances, cabinetry, and finishes of a kitchen can easily make it the most expensive room in a house, an ancient Roman kitchen was the home's most humble space. A shrine to the household gods might be the sole decoration. The location of the kitchen followed no convention. It was discreetly hidden. A stone hearth against one wall, cooking utensils, iron tripods, and perhaps an oven were its most common features. A window or hole in the roof could allow the smoke to escape.

The most conspicuous change over time in the form of the Roman townhouse was the gradual incorporation (beginning in the second century BCE) of a second open space at the back of the house, called the peristyle (*peristylium*). The peristyle was separated from the *atrium* by the *tablinum* and the *alae* (literally, "wings"), which were deep recesses at the back of the *atrium*. The peristyle, a grand and dignified area of the house, took the place of the walled vegetable garden (*hortus*) that had previously been the home's unpretentious backyard. The peristyle consisted of a covered colonnade surrounding an ornamental garden, which would be decorated with statuary in bronze or marble and might be embellished with water features, including fountains. Excepting the presence of picture galleries (*pinacothecae*) displaying panel paintings, only found in the most magnificent homes, the peristyle was the artistic hub of the townhouse. While, with its stone columns, it evoked Greek architecture, its reference point was not Greek houses, but the covered colonnades prominently found in Greek public architecture.

Like the *atrium*, the peristyle brought light and air into the home, but unlike the *atrium* its exposure was extensive—the size of the uncovered garden could be larger than the entire *atrium*. Also like the *atrium*, the peristyle was surrounded by rooms of a much smaller scale. These could include additional *cubicula* and dining rooms. An oversized and ornate dining room, transcending the expectations of a *triclinium*, would instead be referred to as an *oecus*. The crescendo of decoration and overall grandeur as one progressed through a Roman townhouse suggests that access to its deeper recesses was reserved to those participating in or facilitating the most private and privileged encounters.

Villa

Villas were homes in the countryside. *Villa* could refer to a simple farmhouse built to shelter and support agricultural activity. It could equally indicate a structure broadly similar to an upscale townhouse, but tailored to the conditions of rural or suburban life. At their most opulent, *uillae* were the exurban palaces of the Roman emperors. Such versatile application of the term *uilla* to a broad range of dwellings suggests it was not always easy to distinguish a "farmhouse" from a "luxury villa." The countless villas dotting the shoreline and spreading throughout the Italian peninsula beginning in the second century BCE exhibited varying degrees of agricultural productivity and stylish comfort. Furthermore, neither quality necessarily came at the expense of the other, as the *uilla urbana* (residential buildings) could be located discretely from the *uilla rustica* (farming facilities). Pliny the Younger (61–113 CE) thus quips that while one of his villas might yield a full granary, the harvest at another is a full bookcase of manuscripts produced in the comfort of home.[9]

Ancient Roman authors nevertheless identified tensions at the very heart of the *uilla* concept. Villas that exuded rustic simplicity validated the Roman self-image as a nation of disciplined and abstinent farmers with agrarian values. Villas that dazzled by means of precious materials and grand proportions were an affront to this closely cherished idea. Little wonder the Roman agricultural authors Cato the Elder (234–149 BCE), Varro, and Columella (ca. first century CE) expend few words on the amenities that improve a rural home, instead training their focus squarely on the farm and fields. A common solution to inconvenient truths encapsulated by the magnificent villa was to spin a narrative of historical decline, in which an authentically Roman austerity became infiltrated over time by Greek decadence. Varro writes,

> Those great men our ancestors were justified in putting countrified Romans ahead of urbanites. Just as, in the country, those who reside in the villa are lazier than those who are engaged in doing some work on the land, they thought that those who sat around in town were more lethargic than those who cultivated the countryside. [. . .] Nowadays one [exercise ground]

is hardly enough, and people think that they don't have a villa at all unless it positively resounds with Greek names.[10]

One problem, however, with assigning blame to the Greeks was that while some of the vocabulary, materials, decorative motifs, and art associated with Roman villas may have had Greek origins, the luxury villa was a Roman architectural phenomenon without Greek precedent. Villas emerged as a by-product of Rome's conquest of the Mediterranean and the ensuing enslavement of vast numbers of people, whose forced labor enabled the agglomeration of Italian small farms into enormous estates called *latifundia*.

With scores of other people doing the work, the owner could rest, play, and entertain guests. The authors surveyed in this book, including Cicero, Seneca, and Pliny the Younger, portray the atmosphere of the Roman villa as one of relaxation, refinement, and intellectual stimulation. The *uilla urbana* (the very name—literally, "citified villa"—captures a sense of urbane sophistication) was unabashedly designed for pleasure. Its site was carefully chosen to exploit the natural beauty of the landscape or the shoreline. While the plan of the townhouse was oriented inward, with walled interior spaces as the centerpieces, the villa was the inverse: its architec-

ture projected outward by means of open courtyards and far-reaching colonnades on the exterior,
facilitating an interaction between architecture and
nature.

Unlike the Roman townhouse, the villa never
developed a formulaic layout.[11] Vitruvius advises
that the sequence of rooms in a townhouse can be
inverted, so that visitors to a villa enter the peristyle before the *atrium* (see passage 5). The Villa
of the Mysteries, a suburban villa on the outskirts
of Pompeii, adopts this layout, but otherwise it
does not appear to have been the norm. Instead,
villas were sites of architectural experimentation
and innovation. The most striking example of this
is the emperor Hadrian's gigantic villa at Tivoli
(ca. 118–138 CE), where novelties amidst the design
elements (including sculptures of Egyptian croc-
odiles alongside a water feature emulating a canal
off the Nile) gestured at the expansiveness of the
Roman empire. Many villas displayed the greatest
creativity in their landscape architecture, including
ornamental gardens filled with topiaries and parks
where thickets of trees parted to reveal shrines and
gazebos. While manicured landscapes played with
the relationship between artifice and reality, so too
did the wall paintings inside the villa, which sometimes portrayed gardens contiguous with the actual
scenery just steps away. In this way, the villa became

a site for blurring the boundaries between inside and outside. Indeed, even much of the interior architecture was concerned with framing the view.

The extraordinary size of villas, which could easily be tens of thousands of square feet, made them ideal repositories and exhibition spaces for art. Approximately ninety sculptures made of marble or bronze were discovered at the Villa of the Papyri near Herculaneum (buried in 79 CE), the structure of which formed the model for the Getty Villa in Pacific Palisades, California. Much of the ancient sculpture in museums today once ornamented the grounds of Roman villas. These works of art inspired admiration for their aesthetic qualities, cultural connotations, and market value (see passage 12). So deftly integrated into their surroundings were some such collections that the historian Tacitus (56–ca. 120 CE) implies that statue groups could be subsumed within real estate transactions.[12]

Villas were often second (if not third, fourth, or fifth) homes. Cicero seems to have had seven villas, Pliny the Younger at least three or four. Even if the primary purpose of the villa was the recreation of the homeowner, facilities for making wine and oil were expected. Likewise, storerooms and cisterns were essential to villa design. Distance from market staples taken for granted in the city made the self-sustaining, or largely self-sustaining, villa highly desirable (see passage 19). If anything, such storage facilities seem to have increased in scale and number over time: a villa culture based upon frequent buying and selling of goods off-site dwindled as estates grew in size.

Villas were more independent than townhouses in their water supply. Nearby streams could be channeled to serve them (passage 11). By contrast, running water at a townhouse was a special amenity; even a city's wealthier families might be reliant on the public fountains served by aqueducts, rather than enjoying the privilege of pipes entering their homes. Private baths within a townhouse were not necessary, if public facilities were available. Bath facilities, including hot, cool, and warm rooms, as well as swimming pools and saunas, were among the most relaxing features of the villa. As a result, the villa became particularly associated with the luxury (or, for some, the decadence) of bathing at home (passage 17).

Structure of the Volume

The passages translated in this volume have been ordered to create throughlines of subject matter, rather than presented chronologically by author. I begin with stories that conjure up the very origins of domestic architecture. In the first tale, located deep in the mythological past, a pious husband and wife welcome the gods into their humble cottage, the epitome of the morally upright home (Ovid, *Metamorphoses* 8.620–720). A home, however, is not just a representation of its occupants. It is also a product of its culture. The construction of humankind's first hut invites contemplation of how differences across climates and cultures leave their marks on domestic architecture (Vitruvius, *De architectura* 2.1.1–7). Important, too, is the infrastructure that supports the building, maintenance, and occupation of any dwelling (Strabo, *Geographica* 5.3.7–8).

The volume then turns to the question of how homes support and reflect their owners. The design of a Roman house privileges visitor access. Such high exposure suggests that its inhabitants have no shameful secrets (Velleius Paterculus, *Historiae Romanae* 2.13–14). Moreover, there are practical reasons why the houses of the wealthy and powerful must be so open: every home, whether humble or grand, should cater to its occupant's profession, and persons of high status receive many callers (Vitruvius, *De architectura* 1.2.9 and 6.5.1–3). Knowing that a resplendent home carries associations of power and prestige, some proprietors build according to their aspirations, rather than their achievements (Cicero, *De officiis* 1.138–140).

A memorable example of a residence that its owner hardly deserved is the seaside villa of the affluent Servilius Vatia, the ideal setting for a well-deserved retirement, if only Vatia had lived a life of purpose (Seneca, *Epistulae morales* 55.3–8). The behavioral expectations for a man of high station are not difficult to discern: the ancestor portraits on view in his *atrium* embody the standards he should meet in order to be worthy of their display (Juvenal, *Saturae* 8.1–20).

Shifting from the symbolic to the practical, the next set of passages showcases Roman responses to the hazards of home ownership. The dangers and inequities of urban housing are an excellent advertisement for life in the countryside (Juvenal, *Saturae* 3.1–9, 190–229, 268–77). Properties everywhere, however, can be advertised or staged deceptively, precipitating buyer's remorse (Cicero, *De officiis* 3.54–55, 58–61, 65–67). New construction, meanwhile, brings its own headaches, as contractors require on-site supervision (Cicero, *Ad Quintum fratrem* 3.1.1–2, 5–7). Individuals commissioned to purchase art and furnishings (Cicero, *Epistulae ad familiares* 7.23) or to construct a home itself (Vitruvius, *De architectura* 10, preface 1–2) may misjudge in matters of taste, misuse funds, or overspend the budget. Homeowners themselves, however, should not overestimate their own expertise, especially when costly materials are involved (Vitruvius, *De architectura* 7.5.7–8; 7.9.2).

While a grand home with exquisite furnishings can enhance its owner's reputation, lavish building projects and their imported decoration court moral censure. As surely as a stately home can make a career, overindulgence in domestic décor can eat up a fortune, ultimately consigning the structure to rot (Bibaculus, fragments 2 and 1). Such neglect reflects very badly on the proprietor (Plautus, *Mostellaria* 84–156). What, then, is the Roman recipe for success? The ideal home, like its owner, enshrines Roman virtues (Seneca, *Epistulae morales* 86.1–12) and finds the right balance between sparsity and overindulgence (Cornelius Nepos, *Atticus* 13–14). Home, at its best, is not just the backdrop against which we are admired by others, but the promontory from which we gaze upon the wonders of the natural world (Pliny the Younger, *Epistulae* 2.17).

A Note on the Original Languages and These Translations

This volume collates nineteen passages from eleven poets and prose authors. Eighteen are in Latin, and one is in ancient Greek (by an author writing about, and under, the Roman empire). Some passages are in the form of poetry, and others prose. Poetic works have not been rendered in meter. I have attempted, where possible, to preserve some flavor of the varying styles and genres of the various authors.

Readers familiar with the Romans as builders may note with surprise that the words of Vitruvius's *De architectura* (20s BCE), the only work dedicated to architecture that survives from Roman antiquity, represent only a fraction of this book. *De architectura*'s volumes 6 and 7 provide our most detailed ancient account of domestic architecture.[13] However, in keeping with the series' emphasis on wisdom, I have only included selections from *De architectura* that reflect on what these buildings meant, rather than incorporating Vitruvius's full remarks on how homes were designed. The aim of this book is not to describe the forms and spatial logic of Roman architecture, but rather to assemble a collection of ancient commentary on the process of making a home.

The authors surveyed here, virtually all of whom display a general knowledge of philosophy, had no shortage of wisdom. Yet many cautionary tales, both intentional and unwitting, appear within these pages: the values and norms that structured ancient Roman culture were often far different from our own. Casual references to enslavement, as well as to gender and class hierarchies, are common features of ancient Roman texts. I have not altered the use of masculine pronouns (he, him, his) when they appear in generalizations pertinent to ancient men alone, so as to be transparent about the world views the texts relay. Roman women could own and inherit property, yet ancient authors are most concerned with the positive associations of a beautiful home closely tethered to arenas in which women had little or no possibility of participation (most notably, success in politics). It was considered virtuous for an elite Roman woman to stay at home, yet all too often the appearance of this building was viewed as a reflection of her husband's character, rather than her own. The passages of ancient literature that are most vocal about women's roles in "making a home" are concerned with *domestica bona*—the morality that a woman showed by confining herself to household activities (reflections of this appear in passage 1).[14] This brief volume focuses instead on how a home was built, bought, maintained, and decorated. Regrettably, ancient authors tell us very little about how women participated in that (but see passage 12).

The texts here assembled are offered as a stimulus to examine our definitions of style and comfort with fresh eyes, and to consider anew the pleasures and pitfalls of making domestic real estate, construction, renovation, and design cornerstones of self-expression in our own time.

HOW TO MAKE A HOME

1 SIMPLICITY IS BLISS

In the myth of Philemon and Baucis, a simple home epitomizes the humility and religious piety of its occupants. Within its unassuming walls, a mortal husband and wife enjoy the spectacular honor of entertaining the gods on earth. The image of the aging wife Baucis, bowing and scraping to accommodate these otherworldly visitors, offers one of the most detailed (albeit stylized) representations in ancient Roman literature of the domestic activities that occupied many women's daily lives in antiquity. The couple's reciprocal functioning as slave and master to one another, however, evokes gender parity, a concept far at odds with the normative view (pervading much of the surviving evidence) of ancient Roman women as subservient to their husbands. The poet Ovid's (43 BCE–17 CE) use of slavery as a metaphor for another type of relationship, however, is hardly unusual: such invocation of enslavement within a description of a loving marriage testifies to the commonplace acceptance in antiquity of practices recognized as heinously immoral today.

The poetic style of this passage is marked by lofty diction and grammar, which dignify the description of a modest household, made of inexpensive, local materials, into which the lofty figures of the gods themselves enter. Just as Philemon and Baucis are eventually transformed into trees, their cottage is made into a temple, a dazzling ascent of an insubstantial private edifice into a lasting public monument. This architectural metamorphosis not only honors the homeowners, but retroactively justifies the presence of immortals in such a rudimentary structure: ancient Roman temples were designed to function as the houses of the gods themselves.

                    tiliae contermina quercus   620
collibus est Phrygiis, medio circumdata muro.
(ipse locum uidi, nam me Pelopeia Pittheus

misit in arua suo quondam regnata parenti.)
haud procul hinc stagnum est, tellus habitabilis olim,

nunc celebres mergis fulicisque palustribus undae.   625

Iuppiter huc specie mortali cumque parente

uenit Atlantiades positis caducifer alis.

mille domos adiere locum requiemque petentes,

mille domos clausere serae. tamen una recepit,

parua quidem stipulis et canna tecta palustri,   630

sed pia. Baucis anus parilique aetate Philemon

illa sunt annis iuncti iuuenalibus, illa

consenuere casa paupertatemque fatendo

effecere leuem nec iniqua mente ferendo.

Ovid, *Metamorphoses*

In the hills of Phrygia, there stands an oak tree,
joined to a lime tree and surrounded by a low wall.
(I've seen the place myself, because King Pittheus, son
    of Pelops,
sent me to the region his father had once ruled.)[1]
Not far from there is a lake: what once was habitable
    countryside,
now is flowing water, frequented by gulls and
    waterfowl who love the marshes.
Jupiter appeared in this place, disguised as a mortal, and
    along with him
came the grandson of Atlas, the staff bearer,[2] with his
    wings laid aside.
Looking for a place to rest, they approached a
    thousand homes;
a thousand homes had barred the doors against them.
    Nevertheless, one house took them in,
which was truly humble, thatched with straw and
    swamp reed,
but pious.[3] Baucis, an old woman, and Philemon, her
    equal in age,
were wedded in that cottage when they were young,
    and in that cottage
had grown old together, and they alleviated their
    poverty
by acknowledging it, and by bearing it with serenity.

nec refert, dominos illic famulosne requiras: 635

tota domus duo sunt, idem parentque iubentque.

   Ergo ubi caelicolae paruos tetigere Penates

submissoque humiles intrarunt uertice postes,

membra senex posito iussit releuare sedili,

cui superiniecit textum rude sedula Baucis.   640

inde foco tepidum cinerem dimouit et ignes

suscitat hesternos foliisque et cortice sicco

nutrit et ad flammas anima producit anili,

multifidasque faces ramaliaque arida tecto

detulit et minuit paruoque admouit aeno,   645

quodque suus coniunx riguo collegerat horto

truncat holus foliis; furca leuat ille bicorni

sordida terga suis nigro pendentia tigno

There would be nothing to gain from asking about
    masters or slaves in the cottage:
the entire household consisted of two people, each
    obeying and commanding in turn.
      And so, when celestial beings arrived at the humble
        dwelling
and, with heads bowed, entered through the lowly
    doorposts,
the old man, having produced a bench, onto which the
    scrupulous Baucis
threw a makeshift covering, urged them to rest their
    limbs.
Then she swept away the warm ashes on the hearth and
    rekindled the fire
from the day before, and fed it with leaves and dry
    bark,
and with an old woman's breath she summoned it into
    flame.
She took splintered kindling and dry brushwood down
    from the roof,
broke them up, and placed them under the humble
    copper pot.
She pared the leaves of whatever vegetables her
    husband had collected
in their well-watered garden; meanwhile [Philemon]
    with a carving fork
lifted up a meager pork butt, hanging from a blackened
    beam,

seruatoque diu resecat de tergore partem

exiguam sectamque domat feruentibus undis.   650
interea medias fallunt sermonibus horas
sentirique moram prohibent. erat alueus illic

fagineus, dura clauo suspensus ab ansa;
is tepidis impletur aquis artusque fouendos
accipit. in medio torus est de mollibus uluis   655

impositus lecto sponda pedibusque salignis;

uestibus hunc uelant quas non nisi tempore festo

sternere consuerant, sed et haec uilisque uetusque

uestis erat, lecto non indignanda saligno.
accubuere dei. mensam succincta tremensque   660

ponit anus, mensae sed erat pes tertius impar;

testa parem fecit, quae postquam subdita cliuum

sustulit, aequatam mentae tersere uirentes.

ponitur hic bicolor sincerae baca Mineruae

and he cut a small piece from the edge of this long-
saved meat,
chopped it up, and submerged it in the boiling water.
They whiled away the intervening time by chatting
and paid no heed to the delay. Nearby, there was a
beechwood tub
suspended from a nail by a sturdy handle.
This was filled with warm water and used as a footbath.
In the center of the room there was a mattress made of
soft sedge grasses,
positioned on a couch with a framework and legs made
of willow wood.
They overlayed this with a coverlet, which they were
not in the habit of spreading out,
except on holidays; but even this coverlet was of low
quality
and threadbare, well suited to the willow couch.
The gods arranged themselves comfortably on it. The
old woman, trembling,
and with her clothing hiked up, put the table in place.
But one of its three legs was uneven;
so, she evened it out with a fragment of pottery, which,
after having been inserted,
eliminated the slope, and she swabbed the smooth
surface with green mint leaves.
Upon it she placed half-ripened olives, the berries of
truthful Minerva,

conditaque in liquida corna autumnalia faece 665

intibaque et radix et lactis massa coacti
ouaque non acri leuiter uersata fauilla,
omnia fictilibus; post haec caelatus eodem

sistitur argento crater fabricataque fago

pocula, qua caua sunt, flauentibus inlita ceris. 670
parua mora est, epulasque foci misere calentes;

nec longae rursus referuntur uina senectae

dantque locum mensis paulum seducta secundis.

hic nux, hic mixta est rugosis carica palmis

prunaque et in patulis redolentia mala canistris 675
et de purpureis collectae uitibus uuae;
candidus in medio fauus est. super omnia uultus

accessere boni nec iners pauperque uoluntas.

Interea totiens haustum cratera repleri

sponte sua per seque uident succrescere uina; 680

and some autumnal cornelian cherries preserved in the
    lees of wine,
endives, a radish, a hunk of cheese, and eggs,
gently roasted in the warm ashes,
all served on terracotta. After these courses, an
    engraved mixing bowl
of equally costly material was set down, with cups
    made of beechwood
that were coated with yellow wax on the inside.
After a brief delay, the hearth sent forth steaming
    dishes of food, and
the wine, which had not matured for long, was brought
    out again,
and, moving this aside, they made a small space on the
    table for the fruit course.
In it there were nuts, Carian figs commingled with
    wrinkled dates, and
plums, and gaping baskets of fragrant apples,
and purple grapes just picked from the vines;
in the center of the table was a raw comb of clear
    honey. Exceeding all this were the obliging faces
of the hosts, and a goodwill that had nothing crude or
    impoverished about it.
Meanwhile they see that the bowl for mixing wine, as
    many times as it was drained,
became full again spontaneously, as the wine welled up
    on its own.

attoniti nouitate pauent manibusque supinis

concipiunt Baucisque preces timidusque Philemon

et ueniam dapibus nullisque paratibus orant.
unicus anser erat, minimae custodia uillae,

quem dis hospitibus domini mactare parabant;   685

ille celer penna tardos aetate fatigat

eluditque diu tandemque est uisus ad ipsos

confugisse deos. superi uetuere necari

"di" que "sumus, meritasque luet uicinia poenas

impia" dixerunt; "uobis immunibus huius   690

esse mali dabitur. modo uestra relinquite tecta
ac nostros comitate gradus et in ardua montis
ite simul." parent ambo baculisque leuati
nituntur longo uestigia ponere cliuo.

tantum aberant summo quantum semel ire sagitta   695
missa potest; flexere oculos et mersa palude
cetera prospiciunt, tantum sua tecta manere.

Stunned and terrified by this strange novelty, and
  turning the palms of their hands upwards,
Baucis and Philemon began to recite their prayers
  fearfully,
and begged forgiveness for the improvised banquet.
There was one single goose, the guardian of their tiny
  estate,
which they were preparing to butcher, as a sacrifice for
  their divine guests.
Swift-winged, he wore out a couple who were slowing
  down from old age,
and evaded capture for a long time; at last, he appeared
  to flee
for refuge to the gods themselves. The heavenly beings
  forbade that he be killed.
"We are gods," they said. "This wicked community
  will suffer the punishments
they deserve, but you will be exempt from this
  hardship.
Simply leave your home behind, follow our footsteps,
and proceed onto the high peaks of the mountains."
Both complied and, leaning on their walking sticks,
they struggled to place each step they took up the steep
  slope.
When they were a bowshot's distance from the summit,
they cast their eyes around and saw that
every other house was engulfed in swamp, and only
  their own dwelling stood fast.

dumque ea mirantur, dum deflent fata suorum,

illa uetus dominis etiam casa parua duobus

uertitur in templum; furcas subiere columnae,   700

stramina flauescunt aurataque tecta uidentur

caelataeque fores adopertaque marmore tellus.

talia tum placido Saturnius edidit ore:

"dicite, iuste senex et femina coniuge iusto

digna, quid optetis." cum Baucide pauca locutus   705

iudicium superis aperit commune Philemon:

"esse sacerdotes delubraque uestra tueri

poscimus, et quoniam concordes egimus annos,
auferat hora duos eadem, nec coniugis umquam

busta meae uideam neu sim tumulandus ab illa."   710
uota fides sequitur; templi tutela fuere,

donec uita data est. annis aeuoque soluti

While they were awestruck at these houses, and
  weeping abundantly for the fate of
the people they knew, that antiquated cottage of theirs,
  cramped even for its two masters,
was transformed into a temple. Columns replaced the
  split stakes;
the thatch grew yellow, so that the roof appeared
  gilded;
the double doors were emblazoned with relief, the
  ground veiled in marble.
Then with a serene expression Jupiter, son of Saturn,
  said to them:
"Tell us, upstanding old man and wife worthy of such
  an upstanding husband,
what you would like." After he had exchanged a few
  words with Baucis,
Philemon disclosed their communal verdict to the
  heavenly beings:
"We request to become priests, and to safeguard your
  shrines,
and because we have spent our years in harmony,
may the very same hour carry us both off, so that I
  may never see
the grave site of my wife, nor be buried by her."
Their prayers were met with a guarantee. They were
  the protectors of temple,
as long as they lived. Weakened by their years and the
  extent of their lifetime,

ante gradus sacros cum starent forte locique

narrarent casus, frondere Philemona Baucis,

Baucida conspexit senior frondere Philemon.   715

iamque super geminos crescente cacumine uultus

mutua, dum licuit, reddebant dicta "uale"que

"o coniunx" dixere simul, simul abdita texit

ora frutex. ostendit adhuc Thyneius illic

incola de gemino uicinos corpore truncos.   720

while they were standing out in front of the hallowed
    staircase[4] and happened
to be recounting the story of the place, Baucis caught
    sight of Philemon budding leaves;
Philemon, elder of the two, stared back at Baucis
    budding leaves;
and now with the crowns of trees growing above their
    coupled faces,
while they still could, they repeated declarations felt by
    both alike:
"Goodbye, my spouse," they said in unison, and in
    unison bark concealed
their covered mouths. Even now, in that spot,
    Bithynian[5] locals point out
two tree trunks side by side, growing from their
    coupled form.

2 HOW HOUSES CAME TO BE

How did humans first organize themselves into societies? Which inventions expedited this development? Vitruvius (first century BCE) identifies the construction of a primitive hut as a galvanizing moment in the history of humankind: while, in the beginning, early humans find food and shelter in the wild, the discovery of fire creates a domino effect through which people begin to live together and to build ever more advanced structures to shield themselves from the elements. By endowing home construction with such significance, Vitruvius betrays his own ambition to elevate the discipline of architecture to a privileged position within Roman intellectual life and to enhance the significance of his *De architectura* as its foundational text. Vitruvius develops his argument that self-expression through architecture is at the core of the human experience by highlighting differences across the native traditions of various cultures around the Mediterranean basin. It is by analyzing regional variation in house styles, Vitruvius suggests, that we can learn about the relationship between topography and culture.

This passage provided an enduring image of human development that would greatly influence Renaissance humanists and theorists of architecture, including Andrea Palladio and Leon Battista Alberti. It remains to this day the most famous excerpt from Vitruvius's *De architectura*.

Homines uetere more ut ferae in siluis et speluncis et nemoribus nascebantur ciboque agresti uescendo uitam exigebant. interea quodam in loco ab tempestatibus et uentis densae crebritatibus arbores agitatae et inter se terentes ramos ignem excitauerunt et, ea flamma uehementi perterriti, qui circa eum locum fuerunt sunt fugati. postea re quieta propius accedentes cum animaduertissent commoditatem esse magnam corporibus ad ignis teporem, ligna adicientes et id conseruantes alios adducebant et nutu monstrantes ostendebant quas haberent ex eo utilitates. in eo hominum congressu cum profundebantur alitae spiritu uoces, cotidiana consuetudine uocabula ut obtigerant constituerunt, deinde significando res saepius in usu ex euentu fari fortuito coeperunt, et ita sermones inter se procreauerunt.

Ergo cum propter ignis inuentionem conuentus initio apud homines et concilium et conuictus esset natus, et in unum locum plures conuenirent habentes ab natura praemium praeter reliqua animalia ut non proni, sed erecti ambularent mundique et astrorum magnificentiam aspicerent, item manibus et articulis quam uellent rem faciliter tractarent, coeperunt in eo

Vitruvius, *De architectura*

Human beings, in olden times, were born like beasts, in forests and caves and groves, and spent their lives feeding on whatever they had foraged. As time went on, somewhere, trees, densely crowded, tossed by storms and winds and rubbing their branches together, kindled a fire. Terrified by the raging flame, those nearby were chased away. When the conflagration quieted down, approaching nearer, they perceived that the heat of the fire was a great comfort to their bodies. Piling wood on the fire and maintaining it, they began to bring other people close, and gesturing with a nod, they disclosed the advantages they had from it. People in this gathering uttered sounds along with their breath, and day by day they created words, however they happened to form. From then on, assigning names to things often, as a common practice, they began, without even meaning to, to describe events, and they generated conversations amongst themselves accordingly.

Hence, it was because of the discovery of fire that there first arose a convergence of people, the capacity for deliberation, and the phenomenon of living together. More and more people gathered in one place. Since Nature had given them the advantages beyond other animals that they walked, not bending forward, but upright, and looked upon the

coetu alii de fronde facere tecta, alii speluncas fodere sub montibus, nonnulli hirundinum nidos et aedificationes earum imitantes de luto et uirgulis facere loca quae subirent. tunc obseruantes aliena tecta et adicientes suis cogitationibus res nouas, efficiebant in dies meliora genera casarum.

Cum essent autem homines imitabili docilique natura, cotidie inuentionibus gloriantes alius alii ostendebant aedificiorum effectus, et ita exercentes ingenia certationibus in dies melioribus iudiciis efficiebantur. primumque furcis erectis et uirgulis interpositis luto parietes texerunt. alii luteas glaebas arefacientes struebant parietes, materia eos iugumentantes, uitandoque imbres et aestus tegebant harundinibus et fronde. posteaquam per hibernas tempestates tecta non potuerunt imbres sustinere, fastigia facientes, luto inducto proclinatis tectis, stillicidia deducebant.

Haec autem ex is, quae supra scriptae sunt, originibus instituta esse possumus sic animaduertere, quod ad hunc diem nationibus exteris ex his rebus aedificia constituuntur, uti Gallia, Hispania, Lusitania,

magnificence of the world and the stars, and that they easily handled with their hands and fingers whatever they wished, some members of this society began to make dwellings from foliage, others to dig caverns under the hills, and still others, imitating the nests of swallows and their construction methods, made shelters from mud and sticks. After this, observing the homes of strangers and adding new features to their designs, from one day to the next, they produced better kinds of huts.

Since people were of an imitative and teachable nature, they were exhibiting their accomplishments in building to one another every day and boasting of their innovations. Cultivating their talents through rivalry, they incrementally became more astute. At first, with stakes set upright and sticks inserted in between, they fashioned their walls out of mud. Other people constructed walls by drying lumps of mud and binding them with wood, and so as to escape the rain and heat, they covered them with reeds and foliage. When the roofs could not withstand the rains from winter storms, they made pitched roofs and smeared clay on the sloping sides, to draw the rainwater off the eaves.

We can observe that these practices were established from the origins described above, because to this day buildings are constructed from these materials in foreign lands, such as Gaul, Hispania, Lusitania,

Aquitania scandulis robusteis aut stramentis. apud na-
tionem Colchorum in Ponto propter siluarum abun-
dantiam arboribus perpetuis planis dextra ac sinistra
in terra positis, spatio inter eas relicto quanto arborum
longitudines patiuntur, conlocantur in extremis partibus earum supra alterae transuersae quae circum-
cludunt medium spatium habitationis. tum insuper
alternis trabibus ex quattuor partibus angulos iugumentantes, et ita parietes arboribus statuentes ad per-
pendiculum imarum, educunt ad altitudinem turres,
interuallaque quae relinquuntur propter crassitudi-
nem materiae schidiis et luto obstruunt. item tecta,
recidentes ad extremos <angulos> transtra, traiciunt
gradatim contrahentes, et ita ex quattuor partibus
ad altitudinem educunt medio metas, quas fronde et
luto tegentes efficiunt barbarico more testudinata
turrium tecta.

Phryges uero, qui campestribus locis sunt habi-
tantes, propter inopiam siluarum egentes materiae
eligunt tumulos naturales eosque medios fossura dis-
tinentes et itinera perfodientes dilatant spatia, quantum natura loci patitur. insuper autem stipites inter
se religantes metas efficiunt quas harundinibus et sar-
mentis tegentes exaggerant supra habitationes e terra

and Aquitania, with oak shingles or thatch. The Colchians, in Pontus,[1] thanks to the abundance of forests, position two entire tree trunks, having been made level, on the ground to the right and left, with a space left between them as wide as the lengths of the trees allow. At the corners, on top, other tree trunks are placed crosswise, which surround the space in the middle of the dwelling. Then, laying on top of them alternate beams from the four sides, they join up the corners. Constructing the walls with tree trunks in this way, they are able to erect towers that extend perpendicularly from the lowest parts to the full height. The gaps which remain, on account of the thickness of the wood, they block up with wood chips and mud. They convey the roofs across by cutting off the cross-beams at the end and tapering their lengths gradually. And so, from the four sides, they raise conical structures over the middle at the uppermost point. Covering these with foliage and mud, in rough fashion, they construct the coved roofs of their towers.

The Phrygians, who are inhabitants of the level plains and have no timber on account of the absence of forests, opt for natural mounds. After dividing them in the middle by excavating and digging tracks through, they are able to hollow out spaces as large as the nature of the place allows. Tying trunks together at the top, they make conical structures, and

maximos grumos. ita hiemes calidissimas, aestates frigidissimas efficiunt tectorum rationes. nonnulli ex ulua palustri componunt tuguria tecta. apud ceteras quoque gentes et nonnulla loca pari similique ratione casarum perficiuntur constitutiones. non minus etiam Massiliae animaduertere possumus sine tegulis subacta cum paleis terra tecta. Athenis Areopagi antiquitatis exemplar ad hoc tempus luto tectum. item in Capitolio commonefacere potest et significare mores uetustatis Romuli casa et in arce sacrorum stramentis tecta. ita his signis de antiquis inuentionibus aedificiorum, sic ea fuisse ratiocinantes, possumus iudicare.

Cum autem cotidie faciendo tritiores manus ad aedificandum perfecissent et sollertia ingenia exercendo perconsuetudinem ad artes peruenissent, tum etiam industria in animis eorum adiecta perfecit, ut, qui fuerunt in his studiosiores, fabros esse se profiterentur. cum ergo haec ita fuerint primo constituta et natura non solum sensibus ornauisset gentes quemadmodum reliqua animalia, sed etiam cogitationibus et consiliis armauisset mentes et subiecisset cetera

covering these with reeds and brushwood, they pile up very large heaps of earth from the ground on top of their dwellings. In this way, the design of the roofs enables the winters to be very warm, and the summers very cool. Some people construct covered shacks from sedges of the marsh. Among other peoples, also, and in many other places, the layouts of huts are realized according to the same plan or a similar one. Likewise, at Marseille,[2] we can observe roofs without tiles, made of earth and worked through with straw. At Athens, on the Areopagus, there is a replica of ancient construction, to this day covered with mud. On the Capitolium, the Hut of Romulus is able to evoke and illustrate an archaic way of life, as do the straw-roofed shrines on the Citadel.[3] From such examples, we can form our opinions regarding the primeval creation of buildings, since we infer that ancient structures were just like these.

By working daily, people toughened up their hands for building and, by exercising their clever talents, they developed crafts through trial and error. After this, since such diligent activity had enhanced the capacity of their minds, it became possible for people who were more enthusiastic about these activities to profess themselves craftsmen. From such beginnings, Nature not only equipped humankind with perceptions like other animals, but also armed

animalia sub potestate, tunc uero ex fabricationibus aedificiorum gradatim progressi ad ceteras artes et disciplinas, e fera agrestique uita ad mansuetam perduxerunt humanitatem.

Tum autem instruentes animo se ac prospicientes maioribus cogitationibus ex uarietate artium natis, non casas, sed etiam domos fundatas et latericiis parietibus aut e lapide structas materiaque et tegula tectas perficere coeperunt, deinde obseruationibus studiorum e uagantibus iudiciis et incertis ad certas symmetriarum perduxerunt rationes. posteaquam animaduerterunt profusos esse partus naturae ad materiam et abundantem copiam ad aedificationes ab ea comparatam, tractando nutrierunt et auctam per artes ornauerunt uoluptatibus elegantiam uitae.

their minds with ideas and intentions, and subordinated the other animals to their authority. And so, having advanced from the construction of buildings to other crafts and disciplines, they progressed from a wild and rustic life to a domesticated civilization.

Now that they were building up confidence and envisioning grander designs born from the diversity of their crafts, they began to construct, not huts, but houses on foundations, and with brick walls, or built of stone, and with roofs of wood and tiles. Then, drawing upon observations from these pursuits, they passed from wandering and uncertain convictions to the fixed reasoning of symmetry. After they observed that the products of Nature yielded copious materials and provided resources abundantly useful for building, they took care in their handling of them, and they enhanced the refinement of their life, increased as it was by their crafts, with things that brought pleasure too.

3 WHY INFRASTRUCTURE MATTERS

No home is an island, entire of itself (to adapt a phrase from John Donne). Our habitations are only as functional as the infrastructure that supports them. Many Roman homeowners across centuries and throughout the empire enjoyed the privileges of abundant fresh water, expanding trade routes, sanitation, and more. The Roman empire was created and sustained, in large part, by harnessing the potential of emerging technologies in the fields of architecture and engineering. The historian Dionysius of Halicarnassus (ca. 60 BCE–7 BCE) does not damn the Romans with faint praise when he suggests that "the extraordinary greatness of the Roman empire manifests itself above all in three things: the aqueducts, the paved roads, and the construction of drains."[1] The movement of water into and out of cities and settlements was crucial to health, hygiene, nourishment, and the manufacturing of goods, as well as to the hydration of humans, plants, and animals. Likewise, roads, often constructed to facilitate the swift movement of the Roman army, were essential to trade and commerce, religious observance, and many other activities that defined day-to-day life in an interconnected empire.

The Greek author and polymath Strabo (ca. 63 BCE–24 CE), in his seventeen-volume work on geography, applauds the Romans for their preeminence in many fields, ranging from civil engineering to governance. He underscores the pragmatism with which they exploit the natural advantages of the geographic setting of Rome, including the proximity of the city to mines and forests that supply the raw materials for building. Nevertheless, Strabo is eager to stress that the Romans' enjoyment of these advantages is tempered by an unsustainable approach to home construction. Strabo credits his contemporary, the emperor Augustus, with introducing measures to counteract the effects of rampant fires, preventable collapses, and the impulse to build housing higher and higher, in defiance of structural capacity and good sense.

δι᾽ ἣν ἐπὶ τοσοῦτον αὐξηθεῖσα ἡ πόλις ἀντέχει τοῦτο μὲν τροφῇ, τοῦτο δὲ ξύλοις καὶ λίθοις πρὸς τὰς οἰκοδομίας, ἃς ἀδιαλείπτους ποιοῦσιν αἱ συμπτώσεις καὶ ἐμπρήσεις καὶ μεταπράσεις, ἀδιάλειπτοι καὶ αὗται οὖσαι· καὶ γὰρ αἱ μεταπράσεις ἑκούσιοί τινες συμπτώσεις εἰσί, καταβαλλόντων καὶ ἀνοικοδομούντων πρὸς τὰς ἐπιθυμίας ἕτερα ἐξ ἑτέρων. πρὸς ταῦτ᾽ οὖν τό τε τῶν μετάλλων πλῆθος καὶ ἡ ὕλη καὶ οἱ κατακομίζοντες ποταμοὶ θαυμαστὴν παρέχουσι τὴν ὑποχορηγίαν . . . ἐπεμελήθη μὲν οὖν ὁ Σεβαστὸς Καῖσαρ τῶν τοιούτων ἐλαττωμάτων τῆς πόλεως, πρὸς μὲν τὰς ἐμπρήσεις συντάξας στρατιωτικὸν ἐκ τῶν ἀπελευθεριωτῶν τὸ βοηθῆσον, πρὸς δὲ τὰς συμπτώσεις τὰ ὕψη τῶν καινῶν οἰκοδομημάτων καθελών, καὶ κωλύσας ἐξαίρειν ποδῶν ἑβδομήκοντα τὸ πρὸς ταῖς ὁδοῖς ταῖς δημοσίαις. ἀλλ᾽ ὅμως ἐπέλειπεν ἂν ἡ ἐπανόρθωσις, εἰ μὴ τὰ μέταλλα καὶ ἡ ὕλη καὶ τὸ τῆς πορθμείας εὐμεταχείριστον ἀντεῖχε.

Ταῦτα μὲν οὖν ἡ φύσις τῆς χώρας παρέχεται τὰ εὐτυχήματα τῇ πόλει, προσέθεσαν δὲ Ῥωμαῖοι καὶ τὰ ἐκ τῆς προνοίας. τῶν γὰρ Ἑλλήνων περὶ τὰς κτίσεις εὐστοχῆσαι μάλιστα δοξάντων, ὅτι κάλλους ἐστοχάζοντο καὶ ἐρυμνότητος καὶ λιμένων καὶ χώρας εὐ-

Strabo, *Geographica*

This is why the city [of Rome], despite having expanded so much, maintains its advantages, not only with regard to food, but with regard to timber and stone for domestic construction, which the structural collapses and the fires and the re-sales make incessant—and the causes themselves truly are incessant. Moreover, the re-sales, undertaken by people tearing down and building up one house after another, to suit their whim, are akin to voluntary collapses. The multitude of mines, and the timber, and the rivers that convey these materials produce a remarkable supply for this construction [. . .]. Augustus Caesar took charge of addressing Rome's shortcomings along these lines, by organizing a battalion of freed slaves to fight fires and prevent structural collapses and by reducing the height of new buildings and banning construction on public thoroughfares reaching seventy feet or higher; but, all the same, his corrective measures would have failed, if the mines and the timber and the ease of waterborne transportation had not persisted.

So much for the fact that the nature of the place provides benefits to the city; the Romans have also augmented them, and with a purpose; for though the Greeks were especially prone to achieving success in the founding of cities, in that they set their sights

φυοῦς, οὗτοι προὐνόησαν μάλιστα ὧν ὠλιγώρησαν
ἐκεῖνοι, στρώσεως ὁδῶν καὶ ὑδάτων εἰσαγωγῆς καὶ
ὑπονόμων τῶν δυναμένων ἐκκλύζειν τὰ λύματα τῆς
πόλεως εἰς τὸν Τίβεριν. ἔστρωσαν δὲ καὶ τὰς κατὰ
τὴν χώραν ὁδούς, προσθέντες ἐκκοπάς τε λόφων καὶ
ἐγχώσεις κοιλάδων, ὥστε τὰς ἁρμαμάξας δέχεσθαι
πορθμείων φορτία· οἱ δ᾽ ὑπόνομοι συννόμῳ λίθῳ κα-
τακαμφθέντες ὁδοὺς ἁμάξαις χόρτου πορευτὰς ἐνίας
ἀπολελοίπασι. τοσοῦτον δ᾽ ἐστὶ τὸ εἰσαγώγιμον ὕδωρ
διὰ τῶν ὑδραγωγίων, ὥστε ποταμοὺς διὰ τῆς πόλεως
καὶ τῶν ὑπονόμων ῥεῖν, ἅπασαν δὲ οἰκίαν σχεδὸν δε-
ξαμενὰς καὶ σίφωνας καὶ κρουνοὺς ἔχειν ἀφθόνους,
ὧν πλείστην ἐπιμέλειαν ἐποιήσατο Μάρκος Ἀγρίπ-
πας, πολλοῖς καὶ ἄλλοις ἀναθήμασι κοσμήσας τὴν
πόλιν. ὡς δ᾽ εἰπεῖν, οἱ παλαιοὶ μὲν τοῦ κάλλους τῆς
Ῥώμης ὠλιγώρουν, πρὸς ἄλλοις μείζοσι καὶ ἀναγκαι-
οτέροις ὄντες· οἱ δ᾽ ὕστερον καὶ μάλιστα οἱ νῦν καὶ
καθ᾽ ἡμᾶς οὐδὲ τούτου καθυστέρησαν, ἀλλ᾽ ἀναθη-
μάτων πολλῶν καὶ καλῶν ἐπλήρωσαν τὴν πόλιν.

on beauty, a strong position, harbors, and fertile land, the Romans were the most forward thinking in matters that the Greeks cared little about: namely, the paving of roads and the transportation of water, and sewers capable of washing away the filth of the city into the Tiber. And they also laid out roadways throughout the country, leveling the crests of hills and building embankments in the deep valleys, so that their covered carriages convey the freight of ferry boats; and the sewers, vaulted with regular stones, have left some passable routes for wagons of hay. And so much water is imported through the aqueducts that rivers stream through the city and sewers, and almost every house has cisterns, and indoor plumbing, and bounteous watercourses, amenities to which Marcus Agrippa devoted the greatest attention,[2] while he also adorned the city with many other monuments. Almost all the ancient inhabitants were indifferent to the beauty of Rome, as they were engaged in other greater and more necessary matters; whereas their descendants, and especially the Romans now and during my lifetime, have not fallen short in this at all, but instead have filled the city with many attractive monuments.

4 PRIVACY IS FOR NOBODIES

Roman domestic design favored the alignment of the principal rooms of a townhouse along a central axis. A visitor, in other words, could walk from the front door and vestibule through the *atrium* and *tablinum*, to the peristyle with its gardens and colonnade at the back—all without deviating from a straight line (see Introduction and fig. 1). When adopted, this layout gave the house an open feel: a viewer standing at the doorway was afforded a sightline deep into the interior, so long as no doors or other partitions stood in the way.

A Roman townhouse was designed to be accessible to a range of visitors. Since negotiations and transactions at the core of economic, political, and social life commonly took place at home, a loss of "privacy" was probably far from most Romans' minds. Instead, the high visibility of Roman domestic interiors allowed houses to serve as windows into the characters of their occupants: openness to outsiders implied there was nothing to hide, and communicated this politically useful message to anyone who happened to be walking by.

An anecdote recorded by the historian Velleius Paterculus (ca. 19 BCE–after 30 CE) suggests this level of exposure was driven not by architects' preference, but rather by homeowners' demand. The protagonist, Marcus Livius Drusus (d. 91 BCE), was a Roman politician of considerable wealth, who was notorious, according to other sources, for his arrogance and cruelty.[1] Velleius Paterculus, however, preserves an altogether different view of Livius Drusus: that his character was utterly without stain and that, confident in his virtue, he commissioned a house that would capitalize on this political asset. Livius Drusus may have been driven by customs specific to his office of tribune of the *plebs* (the common people) as well: the philosopher and historian Plutarch (ca. 46–119 CE) suggests that, as protectors of the people, Roman tribunes kept their doors open day and night, so that they could offer refuge to those in need.[2]

. . . tribunatum iniit M. Liuius Drusus, uir nobilissi-
mus, eloquentissimus, sanctissimus . . . cuius morum
minime omittatur argumentum. cum aedificaret
domum in Palatio, in eo loco ubi est quae quondam
Ciceronis, mox Censorini fuit, nunc Statilii Sisennae
est, promitteretque ei architectus ita se eam aedifica-
turum ut libera a conspectu immunisque ab omnibus
arbitris esset neque quisquam in eam despicere posset
"tu uero," inquit, "si quid in te artis est, ita compone
domum meam ut, quidquid agam, ab omnibus per-
spici possit."

Velleius Paterculus, *Historiae Romanae*

Marcus Livius Drusus, a man of the highest nobility, the smoothest eloquence, and the most upright virtue, took office as tribune [. . .]. There's an indication of his character that should not be overlooked. When he was building his house on the Palatine, on the site where the house is that once was Cicero's, and later on was Censorinus's, and now is Statilius Sisenna's, the architect guaranteed that he would build it so that it would be free from scrutiny, protected from all onlookers, and that no one could peer down into it. "Really now," [Livius Drusus] replied, "if you have the talent, build my house so that whatever I do can be scrutinized by everyone."

5 A HOME SHOULD REFLECT ITS OWNER

Domestic design and décor were major preoccupations among ancient Romans with the financial means to make their dreams of capacious layouts, intricate designs, and stunning finishes into realities. And yet, throughout the literary record, we encounter the point of view that indulgence in mansion building and high-level interior decoration should be curtailed, limited to those who, in some sense, deserve it. Vitruvius's *De architectura* offers one such set of principles, according to which spaciousness, elegance, and all-around impressiveness are conceived of as professional tools that should only be acquired by those with the capacity to use them.

Alter gradus erit distributionis cum ad usum patrum familiarum et ad pecuniae copiam aut ad eloquentiae dignitatem aedificia aliter disponentur. namque aliter urbanas domos oportere constitui uidetur, aliter quibus ex possessionibus rusticis influunt fructus; non item feneratoribus, aliter beatis et delicatis; potentibus uero quorum cogitationibus res publica gubernatur, ad usum conlocabuntur; et omnino faciendae sunt aptae omnibus personis aedificiorum distributiones.

· · ·

Cum ad regiones caeli ita ea fuerint disposita, tunc etiam animaduertendum est quibus rationibus priuatis aedificiis propria loca patribus familiarum et quemadmodum communia cum extraneis aedificari debeant. namque ex his quae propria sunt, in ea non est potestas omnibus introeundi nisi inuitatis, quemadmodum sunt cubicula, triclinia, balneae ceteraque quae easdem habent usus rationes. communia autem sunt quibus etiam inuocati suo iure de populo possunt uenire, id est uestibula, caua aedium,[1] peristylia quaeque eundem habere possunt usum. igitur is

Vitruvius, *De architectura*

Another level of allocation will be when buildings are designed in accordance with their owners' pursuits, or the extent of their wealth, or the impressiveness of their eloquence. Certainly, urban townhouses should be built in one way, and dwellings for people who earn their money from rural estates in another way; they won't be the same for moneylenders, and they'll be altogether different for the rich and luxuriant. As for the powerful, whose ideas control the state, certainly homes should be adjusted to their purposes. As a matter of fact, in all circumstances, allocations of buildings should be connected to the individuals themselves.

■ ■ ■

When we have designed our plan to take into account the orientation [of the house] to the heavens, then we must direct our attention to how, in private buildings, the rooms belonging to the family and those that are shared with visitors should be built. As for the rooms belonging to the family, such as bedrooms, dining rooms, baths and other areas for similar purposes, no one is allowed to enter these unless invited. The common rooms are those that members of the public can enter at their own prerogative, without being summoned, such as

qui communi sunt fortuna non necessaria magnifica uestibula nec tablina neque atria quod in aliis officia praestant ambiundo neque ab aliis ambiuntur. qui autem fructibus rusticis seruiunt, in eorum uestibulis stabula, tabernae, in aedibus cryptae, horrea, apothecae ceteraque, quae ad fructus seruandos magis quam ad elegantiae decorem possunt esse, ita sunt facienda.

Item feneratoribus et publicanis commodiora et speciosiora et ab insidiis tuta, forensibus autem et disertis elegantiora et spatiosiora ad conuentus excipiundos, nobilibus uero, qui honores magistratusque gerundo praestare debent officia ciuibus, faciunda sunt uestibula regalia, alta atria et peristylia amplissima, siluae ambulationesque laxiores ad decorem maiestatis perfectae; praeterea bybliothecas, pinacothecas, basilicas non dissimili modo quam publicorum operum magnificentia comparatas, quod in domibus eorum saepius et publica consilia et priuata iudicia arbitriaque conficiuntur.

vestibules, *atria*, peristyles and other areas of the same function. Therefore, magnificent vestibules and *atria* and *tablina* are not necessary for those of common circumstances, because they fulfill their duties by soliciting others, and themselves are not solicited.[2] But those who depend upon country produce must have stables and shops in the vestibule, and, within the main building, covered passages, storehouses, wine cellars and other rooms which are necessary for the preservation of produce rather than for a refined appearance.

Similarly, the houses of bankers and tax collectors should be more spacious and outwardly impressive and safe from ambushes, while those for legal advocates and others called upon to make speeches should be both elegant and spacious, so that they can receive assemblies. For the aristocracy, who must hold offices and magistracies and whose duty it is to serve the state, there must be princely vestibules, lofty *atria* and very spacious peristyles, woods and broad walkways completed in a majestic manner; and furthermore, libraries, picture galleries, and basilicas[3] arranged in a similar style, comparable to the magnificence to public structures, because, in the townhouses of these men, public deliberations and private trials and judgments are often transacted.

Ergo si his rationibus ad singulorum generum personas, uti in libro primo de decore est scriptum, ita disposita erunt aedificia, non erit quod reprehendatur; habebunt enim ad omnes res commodas et emendatas explicationes. earum autem rerum non solum erunt in urbe aedificiorum rationes, sed etiam ruri, praeterquam quod in urbe atria proxima ianuis solent esse, ruri ab pseudourbanis statim peristylia, deinde tunc atria habentia circum porticus pauimentatas spectantes ad palaestras et ambulationes.

Therefore, if buildings are designed logically according to the type of individual, as was described in the first book in the discussion of ornament,[4] there will be nothing to criticize. For our directives will be suitable and precise for every scenario. Moreover, this pattern of logic will apply not only for buildings in the city, but also for those in the country; except that, in the city, *atria* are usually close to the front doors and, in the country, the peristyles in dwellings built to look like city homes come first, and from there the *atria* have paved colonnades all around them that overlook the exercise grounds and the promenades.

6 DON'T BE UPSTAGED BY YOUR HOUSE

A majestic home was a visible metric of professional, social, and even political success in ancient Rome. For this reason, a sizable, well-appointed house, designed for entertaining large numbers of guests, could also be used as a tool to enhance the status and prestige of its owner. The orator and statesman Cicero (106–43 BCE), offering recommendations for domestic design specifically tailored to the needs of leading Roman political figures, argues that a house should be constructed and decorated to complement its owner's stature and obligations, rather than to inflate his position in society.

Cicero drives the point home by contrasting the urban residences of two statesmen, Gnaeus Octavius (ca. 245–190 BCE) and Marcus Aemilius Scaurus (ca. 92–52 BCE). After celebrating a naval victory over King Perseus of Macedonia in 168 BCE, Octavius built an impressive home on the northeastern slope of Rome's Palatine hill, financed by the spoils of war. Octavius was careful, however, to balance his private spending with acts of philanthropy: while building this house, he also financed the construction of the Portico of Octavius, which surrounded the Temple of Hercules of the Muses in Rome. It is, for Cicero, a delicious irony that a home that so visibly contributed to Octavius's election to the consulship in 165 BCE would later be demolished by Scaurus, with calamitous repercussions. The grandeur of Scaurus's expanded residence, which boasted columns of Hymettan marble so massive that they would later be repurposed for display in the fifteen-thousand-seat Theater of Marcellus,[1] was no fail-safe against political ruin. Scaurus was prosecuted for extortion and electoral corruption, and eventually exiled from the city of Rome altogether.

Et quoniam omnia persequimur (uolumus quidem
certe), dicendum est etiam qualem hominis honorati
et principis domum placeat esse; cuius finis est usus,
ad quem accommodanda est aedificandi descriptio
et tamen adhibenda commoditatis dignitatisque diligentia. Cn. Octauio, qui primus ex illa familia consul
factus est, honori fuisse accepimus quod praeclaram
aedificasset in Palatio et plenam dignitatis domum,
quae cum uulgo uiseretur suffragata domino, nouo
homini, ad consulatum putabatur. hanc Scaurus demolitus accessionem adiunxit aedibus. itaque ille in
suam domum consulatum primus attulit, hic, summi
et clarissimi uiri filius, in domum multiplicatam non
repulsam solum rettulit sed ignominiam etiam et ca-
lamitatem. ornanda enim est dignitas domo, non ex
domo tota quaerenda, nec domo dominus sed domino domus honestanda est, et, ut in ceteris habenda
ratio non sua solum sed etiam aliorum, sic in domo
clari hominis, in quam et hospites multi recipiendi
et admittenda hominum cuiusque modi multitudo,

Cicero, *De officiis*

Since I am explaining all of this (at least that's my intention), I should also mention what kind of house a respected and distinguished person should have. Usefulness is its objective, and the architectural plan should be tailored to that; all the same, careful attention must be paid to its proportion and stateliness. The story goes that Gnaeus Octavius, who was the first in his family to be made consul,[2] distinguished himself by building a dazzling, and altogether stately, home on the Palatine hill. It was believed to have increased the ballot for its owner, a new man, in his campaign for the consulship, once the general public caught sight of it. This was the house that Scaurus tore down to build an addition onto his own residence. In sum: Octavius brought home a first-generation consulship, while Scaurus, though the son of an eminent and illustrious man, brought back to the same house, once expanded, not just electoral defeat, but public shame and utter ruin. Public standing should be enhanced by a house, rather than procured from it entirely; the owner should dignify the house, not the house the owner. And, as in everything else, one has to take into consideration other people, not just oneself. So, at a prominent person's house, where many guests must be received and crowds of all kinds

adhibenda cura est laxitatis. aliter ampla domus de-
decori saepe domino est, si est in ea solitudo, et maxime si aliquando alio domino solita est frequentari.
odiosum est enim cum a praetereuntibus dicitur:

> o domus antiqua quam dispari
> dominare domino;

quod quidem his temporibus in multis licet dicere.
cauendum autem est, praesertim si ipse aedifices, ne
extra modum sumptu et magnificentia prodeas, quo
in genere multum mali etiam in exemplo est. studiose
enim plerique praesertim in hanc partem facta prin-
cipum imitantur, ut L. Luculli, summi uiri, uirtutem
quis? at quam multi uillarum magnificentiam imitati!
quarum quidem certe est adhibendus modus ad me-
diocritatemque reuocandus. eademque mediocritas
ad omnem usum cultumque uitae transferenda est.

of other people admitted, there should be a great concern for spaciousness. Otherwise, an enormous house is often a discredit to the owner, if there is an emptiness about the place, and especially if at some other time, under a different owner, it was usually thronged. It is offensive, for sure, when passersby comment,

> "O venerable old house! You are owned by such an unworthy owner!"[3]

Nowadays, it's certainly possible to say this about a lot of houses. Caution is advised, especially if you are building for yourself, so that you do not go past the limits of expense and majesty; a lot of harm is done along these lines, if only by the example set. Indeed, a lot of people are eager to imitate the exploits of our leading citizens in that respect: who, for example, imitates the moral valor of Lucius Lucullus, an eminent man? But how many people have imitated the majesty of his villas![4] There absolutely has to be some limit applied to this, and a call back to moderation. And that same moderation should be applied to all the activities and habits in one's life.

7 PRIME REAL ESTATE WON'T SOLVE ALL YOUR PROBLEMS

When a home enables a total withdrawal from society, it is no better than a tomb. Servilius Vatia, a very wealthy man, acquired a reputation for ingeniously evading the violence and chaos of shifting political alliances during the reign of the emperor Tiberius by keeping himself to himself. But the flipside to this strategy of self-preservation was that Vatia's life, bereft of meaningful friendships or impact on his community, served no higher cause. Seneca the Younger (4 BCE–65 CE), himself an enormously rich man, active in the turmoil of court politics as well as the more contemplative realm of philosophy, conveys this impression of Vatia in a letter describing a villa that once belonged to the man. The seaside villa in Cumae, just north of the resort town of Baiae, would be the perfect location for a statesman to enjoy the retirement spent in philosophical study and reflection that comes as a reward for having lived a life of exertion and purpose. But because the occupant was Vatia, the home takes on an altogether different meaning.

The addressee of the letter is Lucilius, the most frequent recipient of Seneca's correspondence, but a person otherwise unknown. Seneca's inability to describe much beyond the facade of the villa, which he glimpses from the road while traveling past it, not only bespeaks the shallowness of Vatia's life, but also enhances the home's resemblance to a tomb: it was a Roman practice to position funerary monuments along major thoroughfares outside of cities, to inspire passersby to remember and reflect on those interred within them.

. . . derexi oculos in uillam quae aliquando Vatiae fuit. in hac ille praetorius diues, nulla alia re quam otio notus, consenuit, et ob hoc unum felix habebatur. nam quotiens aliquos amicitiae Asinii Galli, quotiens Seiani odium, deinde amor merserat (aeque enim offendisse illum quam amasse periculosum fuit), exclamabant homines, "o Vatia, solus scis uiuere." at ille latere sciebat, non uiuere; multum autem interest utrum uita tua otiosa sit an ignaua. numquam aliter hanc uillam Vatia uiuo praeteribam quam ut dicerem, "Vatia hic situs est." sed adeo, mi Lucili, philosophia sacrum quiddam est et uenerabile ut etiam si quid illi simile est mendacio placeat. otiosum enim hominem seductum existimat uulgus et securum et se contentum, sibi uiuentem, quorum nihil ulli contingere nisi sapienti potest. ille solus scit sibi uiuere; ille enim, quod est primum, scit uiuere. nam qui res et homines fugit, quem cupiditatum suarum infelicitas relegauit, qui alios feliciores uidere non potuit, qui uelut timidum atque iners animal metu obliuit, ille sibi non uiuit, sed, quod est turpissimum, uentri, somno, libidini; non continuo sibi uiuit qui nemini. adeo tamen magna res est constantia et in proposito suo perseuerantia ut habeat auctoritatem inertia quoque pertinax.

Seneca, *Epistulae morales*

I cast my eyes over the villa that was once Vatia's. Inside, that wealthy former praetor,[1] not known for anything beyond his recreation, grew old. He was deemed successful for one reason alone, which was that whenever certain people were brought down by their alliances with Asinius Gallus, or others by their hostility towards Sejanus (or in later times their attachment to the latter, since it was equally dangerous to have displeased that man as to have been devoted to him), people used to shout, "O Vatia, only you know how to stay alive!"[2] But he knew how to hide himself away, not how to live; and, in fact, it matters a lot whether your life is completely inactive, or merely unperturbed. I never used to pass by his country house, while Vatia was alive, without commenting, "Here lies Vatia!" More to the point though, my dear Lucilius, is the fact that philosophy is something so worthy to be regarded as divine and commanding of respect, that even the semblance of it is admired. For the general public at large holds the view that a person who has secluded himself is at leisure, and free from anxieties, and self-contained, and lives for himself; none of which can happen for anyone unless he is wise. Only a wise person knows how to live for himself;[3] he even knows the

De ipsa uilla nihil tibi possum certi scribere; frontem enim eius tantum noui et exposita, quae ostendit etiam transeuntibus. speluncae sunt duae magni operis, cuiuis laxo atrio pares, manu factae, quarum altera solem non recipit, altera usque in occidentem tenet. Platanona medius riuus et a mari et ab Acherusio lacu receptus euripi modo diuidit, alendis piscibus, etiam si adsidue exhauriatur, sufficiens. sed illi, cum mare patet, parcitur: cum tempestas piscatoribus dedit ferias, manus ad parata porrigitur. hoc tamen est commodissimum in uilla, quod Baias trans parietem habet: incommodis illarum caret, uoluptatibus fruitur. has laudes eius ipse noui: esse illam totius anni credo; occurrit enim Fauonio et illum adeo excipit ut Bais neget. non stulte uidetur elegisse hunc locum Vatia in quem otium suum pigrum iam et senile conferret.

precondition to it all: how to live. For someone who has fled from responsibilities and people, whom the misfortune of his own desires has banished to seclusion, who cannot see others be happier, who, like an animal scared stiff, has concealed himself because of fear—this person is not living for himself; but for the worst cause of all, that is, for his gluttony, his lethargy, and his lust; a person who lives for no one does not necessarily live for himself. Nevertheless, steadfastness and adherence to one's own purpose is such a lofty goal that even stubborn inactivity commands a certain authority.

In regard to the villa itself, I cannot tell you anything for sure; I am only acquainted with the facade and the areas on display that reveal themselves even to passersby. There are two grottoes, each equal in size to any substantial *atrium*, that have been made by hand, a major feat. One of these is not open to natural light, while the other retains it until the sun sets. A stream running through a grove of plane trees, fed by channels both from the sea and from Lake Acheron, intersects the grove like a trench;[4] it supports the breeding of fish, even though it is regularly siphoned off. When the sea is calm, however, it is not used: but when the storm gives the fishermen a day off, they reach out for what's already at hand. The most advantageous thing about the villa, however, is this: that it has Baiae right next door. It

Sed non multum ad tranquillitatem locus confert: animus est qui sibi commendet omnia. uidi ego in uilla hilari et amoena maestos, uidi in media solitudine occupatis similes.

lacks the disadvantages of that place, while benefiting from its amenities. I am personally acquainted with the merits of the villa, and I believe it is suitable to enjoy year-round. It faces the west wind, and it captures its breezes in a way that Baiae's positioning prevents. Vatia seems to have chosen this location sensibly, as the end-point for his already inactive and decrepit retirement.

Location, however, does not contribute much to peace of mind; it is the mind that can make everything agreeable to itself. I have seen people gloomy in a cheerful and lovely villa; I have seen people looking preoccupied in the midst of solitude.

8 DISPLAYING PORTRAITS OF YOUR ANCESTORS COULD MAKE YOU LOOK SHABBY

The *atrium*, with its open ceiling allowing the entry of light and air, and the collection of rain water, was at the front and center of a Roman townhouse, both spatially and symbolically. It was also the area of the home that looked most emphatically to the past. The *atrium* was closely associated with the hearth, whether or not fires were still kindled there, as well as the ancestral origins of the individual who owned the residence. Visitors to a Roman townhouse, for whom the *atrium* often served as a waiting room, might be introduced to deceased members of the family before living ones, since ancestor portraits were prominently displayed there. Such images, which could take the form of masks, paintings, reliefs, figurines, statues, or busts, might be made of wax, wood, or stone. Many of these likenesses, including the wax masks that seem to have closely captured the sitter's facial features, were created while the subject was alive. Displayed in aggregate, these images served to indicate deep origins within the Roman aristocracy, whether or not the family in question was included among the narrow scope of patrician families that had once comprised the elite.

These bloodlines, and the veneration they inspired, had concrete political implications, in addition to whatever social or emotional significance they might carry. While upward mobility was a more prominent phenomenon within the Roman class system than in those of many other ancient Mediterranean societies, hereditary nobility remained an abiding feature of Roman social consciousness and status hierarchies. This notion had been especially vibrant during the Roman Republic, when nobility (*nobilitas*) could be variously defined, but most often denoted descent from a consul (one of two chief magistrates at Rome, elected annually), or at the very least a high-office holder. One of the most visible manifestations of *nobilitas* in society was the display of ancestor portraits, both as a feature of home décor and as an element of costuming for aristocratic funerals.

The opening of a satire by the poet Juvenal (late first to early second century CE) makes the case that unless a homeowner has behaved nobly, an *atrium* full of ancestor portraits functions as a reproach, rather than a badge of honor. References to military achievements and political offices pile up in line after line of the poem, creating a verbal shrine to elite masculinity, as defined by its manifestation in deeds. The idea that there was a truer sense of nobility achieved by actions, rather than family ties, was no innovation on Juvenal's part: questioning the notion of hereditary nobility was a mainstay of Roman intellectual thought.

8.1–20

Stemmata quid faciunt? quid prodest, Pontice, longo

sanguine censeri, pictos ostendere uultus

maiorum et stantis in curribus Aemilianos

et Curios iam dimidios umeroque minorem

Coruinum et Galbam auriculis nasoque carentem,
[quis fructus generis tabula iactare capaci

censorem, posthac multa contingere uirga

fumosos equitum cum dictatore magistros,]

si coram Lepidis male uiuitur? effigies quo

tot bellatorum, si luditur alea pernox

ante Numantinos, si dormire incipis ortu

luciferi, quo signa duces et castra mouebant?

cur Allobrogicis et magna gaudeat ara

Juvenal, *Saturae*

Family trees: what do they achieve? What good does it
    do, Ponticus,[1]
to be admired for a distant bloodline, to put on display
    painted portraits
of your ancestors, Aemiliani positioned upright in their
    chariots,
and Curii now split in two, a Corvinus missing a
    shoulder,
and a Galba lacking his ears and nose?[2]
What is to be gained from brandishing the censor on an
    enormous
genealogical chart, and after that of reaching through
    many branches
towards smoke-covered lieutenant dictators, along with
    a dictator himself,[3]
if one lives badly when face to face with the Lepidi?
    What's the point
of so many statues of warriors, if there is gambling all
    night
in the presence of the Numantini, if you go to sleep as
    the morning star rises,
when those generals were advancing their standards
    and camps?
Why should a Fabius born in Hercules's line take
    pleasure

natus in Herculeo Fabius lare, si cupidus, si

uanus et Euganea quantumuis mollior agna,

si tenerum attritus Catinensi pumice lumbum

squalentis traducit auos emptorque ueneni

frangenda miseram funestat imagine gentem?

tota licet ueteres exornent undique cerae

atria, nobilitas sola est atque unica uirtus.

in the Allobrogici and the Great Altar, if he is full of
    desire, if
he is untrustworthy—and meeker, to some degree, than
    a Euganean lamb,
if having shaved his groin smooth with Catanian
    pumice,
he mortifies his scruffy forefathers,[4] and if his poison-
    mongering pollutes his miserable
family group through the addition of a statue worthy
    of being broken to pieces?
It's all well and good for wax portraits from long ago to
    garnish *atria*
in every nook and cranny; the one and only nobility is
    moral valor.

9 UNLESS YOU HAVE DEEP POCKETS, THE BIG CITY IS A DEATH TRAP

The contrast between city and country was a major preoccupation for Roman authors. While the countryside was the hub of leisure activities, intellectual pursuits, and relaxed socializing, the city (and especially Rome itself) bore associations of business and politics. Romans with the means to do so (or traveling in the entourage of those who had such means), often split their time between urban and rural settings. Each side of this duality had its pleasures, as well as its shortcomings. Juvenal invokes this theme in a poem lamenting his friend Umbricius's departure from the city of Rome for Cumae, near the Bay of Naples. The first section of the poem excerpted here is spoken in the voice of the poet, and the second and third are quoted from Umbricius's reply, which lampoons the inequities, dangers, and humiliations of city life as justification for withdrawal.

3.1–9, 190–229, 268–277

Quamuis digressu ueteris confusus amici
laudo tamen, uacuis quod sedem figere Cumis

destinet atque unum ciuem donare Sibyllae.

ianua Baiarum est et gratum litus amoeni
secessus. ego uel Prochytam praepono Suburae;   5

nam quid tam miserum, tam solum uidimus, ut non

deterius credas horrere incendia, lapsus

tectorum adsiduos ac mille pericula saeuae

urbis et Augusto recitantes mense poetas?

■ ■ ■

quis timet aut timuit gelida Praeneste ruinam   190

aut positis nemorosa inter iuga Volsiniis aut

simplicibus Gabiis aut proni Tiburis arce?

nos urbem colimus tenui tibicine fultam
magna parte sui; nam sic labentibus obstat

Juvenal, *Saturae*

Although I am distraught at my old friend's departure,
nevertheless, I applaud his decision to make his home
　　at the abandoned town of Cumae,
and to consign himself to the Sibyl, to be her lone
　　fellow-citizen there.
Cumae is the gateway to Baiae, an appealing coastline
with pleasant seclusion. I myself prefer even Prochyta
　　to the Subura.[1]
After all, what place have you ever seen that is so
　　depressing and desolate that
you wouldn't consider it worse to live in fear of fires,
　　and the
continual collapsing of buildings, and the thousand
　　other dangers
of the cruel city of Rome—even poets reciting in the
　　month of August?[2]

■ ■ ■

Does anyone right now fear, or really has anyone ever
　　feared,
buildings falling down at cool Praeneste or at Volsinii
　　among its
well-forested cliffs or at simple Gabii or on the hilltop
　　of gently sloping Tivoli?[3]
We dwell in a city propped up by spindly piers,
for the most part. That's the way the property manager
　　stops structures

uilicus et, ueteris rimae cum texit hiatum,   195

securos pendente iubet dormire ruina.
uiuendum est illic, ubi nulla incendia, nulli

nocte metus. iam poscit aquam, iam friuola transfert

Ucalegon, tabulata tibi iam tertia fumant:

tu nescis; nam si gradibus trepidatur ab imis,   200

ultimus ardebit quem tegula sola tuetur

a pluuia, molles ubi reddunt oua columbae.

lectus erat Cordo Procula minor, urceoli sex

ornamentum abaci, nec non et paruulus infra

cantharus et recubans sub eodem marmore Chiron,   205
iamque uetus Graecos seruabat cista libellos

et diuina opici rodebant carmina mures.

nil habuit Cordus, quis enim negat? et tamen illud

perdidit infelix totum nihil. ultimus autem

from tumbling down. When he has concealed the
    opening of a long-standing fissure,
he coaxes us to sleep tight inside a pending collapse.
The place to live is somewhere without fires, or
    anxieties for one's safety,
at night. Ucalegon is already shouting "Fire!," already
    hauling away his junk,
and the third floor, for your information, is already
    smoking.
But you are completely unaware. After all, if the alarm
    is raised at the bottom of the stairs,
the last to burn will be the person shielded from the
    rain
by a single roof tile, under which soft doves lay their
    eggs.[4]
Cordus had a bed too small for Procula,[5] six little
    pitchers
as decoration for his sideboard, and, below, a puny
    drinking vessel
and a reclining Chiron, made from the same marble,
and a wicker box, now ancient, which conserved his
    little Greek books,
even as uneducated mice nibbled on the divine poetry.

Cordus had nothing, who would disagree?
    Nevertheless,
the unlucky fellow lost all that nothing. But the
    pinnacle

aerumnae cumulus, quod nudum et frusta rogantem   210

nemo cibo, nemo hospitio tectoque iuuabit.

si magna Asturici cecidit domus, horrida mater,

pullati proceres, differt uadimonia praetor.

tum gemimus casus urbis, tunc odimus ignem.

ardet adhuc, et iam accurrit qui marmora donet,   215

conferat inpensas; hic nuda et candida signa,

hic aliquid praeclarum Euphranoris et Polycliti,
haec Asianorum uetera ornamenta deorum,

hic libros dabit et forulos mediamque Mineruam,

hic modium argenti. meliora ac plura reponit   220

Persicus orborum lautissimus et merito iam

suspectus tamquam ipse suas incenderit aedes.

si potes auelli circensibus, optima Sorae

aut Fabrateriae domus aut Frusinone paratur

of his suffering is the fact that when he is naked and
    begging for a morsel to eat,
no one will help him with food or neighborly kindness
    or shelter. If, on the other hand,
the fabulous home that once was Asturicus's falls
    down, then the lady of the house
tears her hair out, the ruling class are in mourners'
    dress, and the praetor postpones his hearings.
That's when we bemoan Rome's downward plunge and
    that's when we loathe the fires.
Even as that house is burning, someone is already
    rushing up to donate marble
or contribute building materials. Someone's about to
    give gleaming nude statues,
and another a famous work of Euphranor or Polyclitus;
someone will give heirloom adornments of the Asian
    gods,
another will give books and bookshelves and a Minerva
    centerpiece,
and another a quantity of silver plate. Persicus, the
    most opulent of all childless people,
replaces his belongings with those that are better and
    more plentiful.
And quite rightly he is now suspected of deliberately
    setting fire to his own house.
If you can tear yourself away from the racetrack, a
    wonderful house
at Sora or Fabrateria or Frusino[6] can be bought for the
    amount

quanti nunc tenebras unum conducis in annum.   225
hortulus hic puteusque breuis nec reste mouendus

in tenuis plantas facili diffunditur haustu.
uiue bidentis amans et culti uilicus horti

unde epulum possis centum dare Pythagoreis.

■ ■ ■

respice nunc alia ac diuersa pericula noctis:
quod spatium tectis sublimibus unde cerebrum
testa ferit, quotiens rimosa et curta fenestris   270

uasa cadant, quanto percussum pondere signent

et laedant silicem. possis ignauus haberi
et subiti casus inprouidus, ad cenam si

intestatus eas: adeo tot fata, quot illa

nocte patent uigiles te praetereunte fenestrae.   275

ergo optes uotumque feras miserabile tecum,

ut sint contentae patulas defundere pelues.

THE BIG CITY IS A DEATH TRAP

you currently pay yearly to rent an unlit room.
There is a little garden and a well shallow enough that a
    rope is unnecessary,
since water is easily drawn to wet the tender seedlings.
Live there, enamored of your weeding fork, and be
    property manager to your vegetable garden,
which will enable you to host a banquet for a hundred
    Pythagoreans.[7]

■ ■ ■

Now consider various other dangers of the night.
Way up high are the towering roofs from which a tile
smacks your skull, how often cracked and broken
    containers plummet
from windows! With what force they lacerate and
    break apart the pavement
when they smash! You can be considered irresponsible
and oblivious to the possibility of accidents if you go
    out to dinner
without having made your will. As you pass by at
    night, there are as many
causes of death as there are windows lying open like
    watchful eyes.
Therefore, say a prayer and continue that pathetic plea
    as you go,
so that people will be satisfied with merely emptying
    their gaping chamber pots on you.

10 CAVEAT EMPTOR

Potential homeowners in ancient Rome were wise to heed the warning, "Let the buyer beware." Properties offered for sale, then as now, could be staged to conceal defects or advertise bogus attributes. Cicero's *De officiis* (On duties), a work outlining appropriate behavior, provides colorful anecdotes of real-estate purchases gone wrong. The three excerpts reproduced below are drawn from *De officiis*'s third book, a volume partly concerned with economic matters. Each offers a window into how sellers' deceptions corrupted the housing market. In the first, the Greek philosophers Diogenes and Antipater, historical figures of the second century BCE for whom Cicero scripts an imagined conversation, debate the ethics of information asymmetry (withholding knowledge of a home's defects).

The second and third excerpts present case studies of individuals on the wrong end of fraud (the former) and information asymmetry (the latter). Each story ends on a sour note, as the injured party has no recourse to legal protection. However, by the time Cicero published *De officiis*, as the author acknowledges, the contractual rights of Romans buyers were better protected.

Vendat aedes uir bonus propter aliqua uitia quae ipse norit, ceteri ignorent, pestilentes sint et habeantur salubres, ignoretur in omnibus cubiculis apparere serpentes, male materiatae <sint et> ruinosae, sed hoc praeter dominum nemo sciat; quaero, si haec emptoribus uenditor non dixerit aedesque uendiderit pluris multo quam se uenditurum putarit, num id iniuste aut improbe fecerit? "ille uero," inquit Antipater. "quid est enim aliud erranti uiam non monstrare, quod Athenis exsecrationibus publicis sanctum est, si hoc non est, emptorem pati ruere et per errorem in maximam fraudem incurrere? plus etiam est quam uiam non monstrare; nam est scientem in errorem alterum inducere." Diogenes contra: "num te emere coegit qui ne hortatus quidem est? ille quod non placebat proscripsit, tu quod placebat emisti. quod si qui proscribunt uillam bonam beneque aedificatam non existimantur fefellisse, etiamsi illa nec bona est nec aedificata ratione, multo minus qui domum non laudarunt. ubi enim iudicium emptoris est, ibi fraus uenditoris quae potest esse? sin autem dictum non omne praestandum est, quod dictum non est, id praestandum putas? quid uero est stultius quam uenditorem eius rei quam uendat uitia narrare? quid autem tam absurdum quam si domini iussu ita praeco praedicet: 'domum pestilentem uendo?'"

Let's say a respected man is selling a house because of certain flaws, which he himself knows, but which other people know nothing about. Let's say it harbors disease, but is considered hygienic, and that the evidence of maggots in all the bedrooms is not well known. Let's say it was constructed from shoddy lumber and is liable to collapse, but no one knows this beyond the owner. I ask, if the seller does not tell the buyers these things and sells the house for far more than thought he would, will he be acting unfairly or improperly? "Yes, he will," says Antipater, "to allow a buyer to blunder ahead and encounter grave harm by mistake: if this is not declining to give directions to someone who is lost, which at Athens is punished by public denunciation, what is? It is even more than declining to give directions; it is enticing someone into a deliberate error." Diogenes said in reply, "Someone who didn't even encourage you hardly forced you to buy it, did he? He posted an advertisement for something he did not like; you bought something you did. But if people who advertise a 'fine, well-built villa' aren't considered deceitful, even though the villa is neither fine nor soundly constructed, far less deceitful are those who did not praise the home at all. Wherever there is buyer's

■ ■ ■

C. Canius, eques Romanus nec infacetus et satis litter-
atus, cum se Syracusas otiandi, ut ipse dicere solebat,
non negotiandi causa contulisset, dictitabat se hortulos aliquos emere uelle, quo inuitare amicos et ubi
se oblectare sine interpellatoribus posset. quod cum
percrebruisset, Pythius ei quidam, qui argentariam
faceret Syracusis, uenales quidem se hortos non habere, sed licere uti Canio, si uellet, ut suis, et simul
ad cenam hominem in hortos inuitauit in posterum
diem. cum ille promisisset, tum Pythius, qui esset ut
argentarius apud omnes ordines gratiosus, piscatores
ad se conuocauit, et ab iis petiuit ut ante suos hortulos
postridie piscarentur, dixitque quid eos facere uellet.
ad cenam tempori uenit Canius; opipare a Pythio
apparatum conuiuium, cumbarum ante oculos multitudo, pro se quisque quod ceperat adferebat; ante
pedes Pythi pisces abiciebantur. tum Canius "quaeso,"

discretion, how can there be seller's fraud? But if, on the contrary, every remark does not need to be answered for, do you think what's unremarked upon must be answered for? In all honesty, what's stupider than a seller describing the flaws of the very thing that he sells? And furthermore, what would be as preposterous as an auctioneer announcing, at an owner's bidding: 'I am promoting the sale of a disease-ridden house?'"

■ ■ ■

Gaius Canius,[1] a Roman of the equestrian order,[2] who was clever and fairly cultured, once went to Syracuse for pleasure (as he used to say), rather than for business. There, he kept talking about how he wanted to buy a little country estate, where he could invite friends and enjoy himself, without unwelcome guests. When this became widely known, a certain Pythius,[3] who had set up a banking business at Syracuse, told him that that he did not have any such estate for sale, but that Canius, if he wished, might enjoy his as his own; and in the same breath he invited the man for dinner at his estate the next day. After Canius accepted the invitation, Pythius, who as a banker enjoyed influence among people of every station in life, summoned the fishermen to him, and asked them to do the next day's fishing in front of his estate, and told them what he wanted

inquit, "quid est hoc, Pythi? tantumne piscium? tantumne cumbarum?" et ille "quid mirum?" inquit. "hoc
loco est Syracusis quidquid est piscium, hic aquatio,
hac uilla isti carere non possunt." incensus Canius cu-
piditate contendit a Pythio ut uenderet. grauate ille
primo. quid multa? impetrat. emit homo cupidus et
locuples tanti quanti Pythius uoluit, et emit instruc-
tos. nomina facit, negotium conficit. inuitat Canius
postridie familiares suos, uenit ipse mature, scalmum
nullum uidet. quaerit ex proximo uicino num feriae
quaedam piscatorum essent, quod eos nullos uideret.
"nullae, quod sciam," inquit ille, "sed hic piscari nulli
solent. itaque heri mirabar quid accidisset." stomach-
ari Canius, sed quid faceret?

Nondum enim C. Aquilius, conlega et familiaris
meus, protulerat de dolo malo formulas; in quibus
ipsis, cum ex eo quaereretur quid esset dolus malus,

them to do. Canius came to dinner on time; the dinner party was luxuriously appointed, thanks to Pythius; before their eyes was a fleet of skiffs; each fisherman brought forward what he himself had caught; and the fish were thrown at the feet of Pythius. Then Canius said, "Pythius, please tell me what this means—all these fish?—all these skiffs?" And Pythius replied, "What's the surprise? This is where all the fish in Syracuse are; this is the source of fresh water; those guys can't be kept away from this villa." Inflamed with eagerness, Canius begged Pythius to sell it. Pythius was reluctant at first. Why drag it out? Canius got his way. Being both eager and rich, he paid as much as Pythius wanted; and he bought it fully furnished. Pythius entered the transaction into the ledger and completed the deal. On the following day, Canius invited his friends; he arrived early himself, and he caught sight of not even the pin to attach an oar. He enquired from the nearest neighbor whether there was some fishermen's holiday, since he could see none of them at all. "Not that I know of," he said, "but none of them are accustomed to fish here. And so yesterday I was wondering what had happened." Canius boiled with rage, but what could he do?

My colleague and close friend Gaius Aquilius had not yet put forward the legal formulae relating to bad faith.[4] When he was asked what the "bad

respondebat cum esset aliud simulatum, aliud actum.
hoc quidem sane luculente, ut ab homine perito
definiendi. ergo et Pythius et omnes aliud agentes,
aliud simulantes perfidi improbi malitiosi. nullum igitur eorum factum potest utile esse, cum sit tot uitiis
inquinatum. quod si Aquiliana definitio uera est, ex
omni uita simulatio dissimulatioque tollenda est. ita
nec ut emat melius nec ut uendat quicquam simulabit
aut dissimulabit uir bonus.

■ ■ ■

Ut, cum in arce augurium augures acturi essent ius-
sissentque T. Claudium Centumalum, qui aedes in
Caelio monte habebat, demoliri ea quorum altitudo
officeret auspiciis, Claudius proscripsit insulam [uen-
didit]. emit P. Calpurnius Lanarius. huic ab auguribus
illud idem denuntiatum est. itaque Calpurnius cum
demolitus esset cognossetque Claudium aedes postea
proscripsisse quam esset ab auguribus demoliri ius-
sus, arbitrum illum adegit QUICQUID SIBI DARE
FACERE OPORTERET EX FIDE BONA. M. Cato
sententiam dixit, huius nostri Catonis pater (ut enim
ceteri ex patribus, sic hic, qui illud lumen progenuit, ex
filio est nominandus): is igitur iudex ita pronuntiauit,

faith" indicated in these formulae was, he used to respond, "Feigning one thing, and doing another." This is an elegant and sensible definition, as one might anticipate from an expert. Pythius and all the other people who do one thing, while feigning another, therefore are treacherous, unethical, and malicious. Nothing they have done can be of any value, since it is tainted by so many flaws. But if Aquilius's definition is right, pretense and deceit should be eliminated from every part of life. In this way, a respectable man won't feign or deceive so that he can buy or sell something at greater advantage.

■ ■ ■

For example, when the augurs were proposing to take observations from the citadel and they ordered Tiberius Claudius Centumalus, who had a house on the Caelian hill, to demolish the parts of it that were tall enough to block the observation of omens from birds, Claudius advertised the building for sale.[5] Publius Calpurnius Lanarius bought it.[6] The same notice was served to him by the augurs. So, when Calpurnius had done the demolition and found out that Claudius had advertised the house for sale after he had been ordered by the augurs to pull part of it down, he compelled him to appear before an arbitrator to determine "what the owner

cum in uendendo rem eam scisset et non pronuntiasset, emptori damnum praestari oportere. ergo ad fidem bonam statuit pertinere notum esse emptori uitium quod nosset uenditor.

would be required to render or pay to him in good faith." Marcus Cato, father to the Cato we know,[7] gave the verdict (just as other people receive names from their fathers, this man, who brought such brilliance into the world, must receive name recognition from his son); anyway, Marcus Cato, acting as judge, decided the case in this way: "Since the seller had known this information while promoting the sale and not disclosed it, the financial loss to the buyer must be made good." In so doing, he established the principle that it was a matter of good faith that any flaw known to the seller be known to the buyer.

11 NEW CONSTRUCTION REQUIRES YOUR PRESENCE AND INPUT

Building a new home brings its own challenges, as crucial decisions that will affect the structure's soundness, functionality, and beauty arrive hard and fast. In September of 54 BCE, Cicero wrote a letter to his brother Quintus, reporting on construction at some of Quintus's villas south of Rome. As Cicero's account progresses, the prospect of any swift completion to one project fades: the foreman Diphilus is exasperatingly slow; meanwhile, lopsided columns must be taken down. Cicero asserts himself as a guiding presence whose involvement is essential. His decisiveness sends a clear message: without having seen the construction site with his own eyes, Quintus is in no position to quibble with his older brother's resolve.

Ego ex magnis caloribus (non enim meminimus
maiores) in Arpinati summa cum amoenitate flumi-
nis me refeci ludorum diebus, Philotimo tribulibus
commendatis.

In Arcano a.d. iiii Id. Sept. fui. ibi Mescidium cum
Philoxeno aquamque, quam ii ducebant non longe a
uilla, belle sane fluentem uidi, praesertim maxima sic-
citate, uberioremque aliquanto sese collecturos esse
dicebant. apud Herum recte erat.

In Maniliano offendi Diphilum Diphilo tardio-
rem. sed tamen nihil ei restabat praeter balnearia et
ambulationem et auiarium. uilla mihi ualde placuit
propterea quod summam dignitatem pauimentata
porticus habebat, quod mihi nunc denique apparuit
postea quam et ipsa tota patet et columnae politae
sunt. totum in eo est, quod mihi erit curae, tectorium
ut concinnum sit. pauimenta recte fieri uidebantur;
cameras quasdam non probaui mutarique iussi.

Cicero, *Ad Quintum fratrem*

Right after the heat wave—I don't remember any hotter—I restored my well-being at the villa at Arpinum,[1] thanks to the unsurpassed pleasantness of the river, during the days of the games, after I entrusted my fellow tribesmen to Philotimus's care.[2]

I was at Arcanum on the tenth of September. There I saw Mescidius with Philoxenus, and the water, which they were channeling not far from your villa, streaming quite nicely, especially given the severe drought, and they said that they were about to accumulate copious amounts more. All was well with Herus.

At your Manilian property,[3] I bumped into Diphilus, outdoing himself in sluggishness.[4] But still, there was nothing left for him to do beyond the baths, and a walkway, and an aviary. I liked the villa very much, because its paved colonnade was extremely impressive, and at last I was able to witness both that the colonnade itself is open to access and that the columns have a high gloss. It all comes down to this (and this is the object of my concern): that the stucco work be neatly done. The pavements appeared to be being laid out correctly. I did not approve of some of the vaulted ceilings, and ordered them to be changed.

Quo loco in porticu te scribere aiunt ut atriolum fiat, mihi ut est magis placebat. neque enim satis loci uidebatur esse atriolo neque fere solet nisi in iis aedificiis fieri in quibus est atrium maius nec habere poterat adiuncta cubicula et eius modi membra. nunc hoc uel honestae testudinis uel ualde boni aestiui locum obtinebit. tu tamen si aliter sentis, rescribe quam primum.

In balneariis assa in alterum apodyteri angulum promoui propterea quod ita erant posita ut eorum uaporarium [ex quo ignis erumpit] esset subiectum cubiculi<s>. subgrande cubiculum autem et hibernum alt<er>um ualde probaui quod et ampla erant et loco posita ambulationis uno latere, eo quod est proximum balneariis. columnas neque rectas neque e regione Diphilus collocarat; eas scilicet demolietur. aliquando perpendiculo et linea discet uti. omnino spero paucis mensibus opus Diphili perfectum fore. curat enim diligentissime Caesius, qui tum mecum fuit.

■ ■ ■

Nicephorum, uilicum tuum, sane probaui quaesiuique ex eo ecquid ei de illa aedificatiuncula Laterii

They say that you wrote that there should be a small *atrium* in that part of the colonnade. I like it better just as it is. Certainly, there did not seem to be enough space for a small *atrium*, nor is it the usual practice to have one, except in those buildings in which there is a larger *atrium*; and it could not have bedrooms and rooms like that alongside it. As it is now, there is room either for a proper vaulted chamber or a good summer room, surely. However, if you think otherwise, write back as soon as possible.

In the bath complex, I have moved the sauna to the other corner of the changing room, because it was so placed that its steam-pipe, from which fire shoots out, was positioned under the bedrooms. A largish bedroom and the other winter room I enthusiastically approved, since they were both spacious and well situated on the side of the walkway that is nearest to the bath complex. Diphilus had set up the columns neither perpendicular, nor in a straight line; these, of course, he will pull down; at some point he will learn to use a plumb line and cord. All told, I hope Diphilus's work will be completed in a few months: after all, Caesius, who was with me then, is attending to that most scrupulously.

■ ■ ■

I utterly approve of your property manager Nicephorus. I asked him whether you had given

de qua mecum locutus es mandauisses. tum is mihi respondit se ipsum eius operis HS $\overline{XVI}$ conductorem fuisse, sed te postea multa addidisse ad opus, nihil ad pretium; itaque id se omisisse. mihi mehercule ualde placet te illa ut constitueras addere; quamquam ea uilla quae nunc est tamquam philosopha uidetur esse quae obiurget ceterarum uillarum insaniam. uerum tamen illud additum delectabit. topiarium laudaui. ita omnia conuestiuit hedera, qua basim uillae, qua intercolumnia ambulationis, ut denique illi palliati topiariam facere uideantur et hederam uendere. iam ἀποδυτηρίῳ nihil alsius, nihil muscosius.

Habes fere de rebus rusticis. urbanam expolitionem urget ille quidem [et] Philotimus et Cincius, sed etiam ipse crebro interuiso, quod est facile factu. quam ob rem ea te cura liberatum uolo.

him instructions regarding that little bit of building at Laterium about which you had spoken to me. He replied that he himself had been contracted for the project at the price of 16,000 sesterces, but that afterward you had added a great deal to the project, but nothing to the price, so he had abandoned it. I am very strongly in favor of the elements you had proposed to add, even though your villa, as it is now, seems philosophical, so to speak, in the way that it offers a rebuke to the mad extravagance of other villas. But still, that addition will be delightful. I commended the landscape gardener. He has cloaked everything in ivy, extending as far as the foundation of the house and the spaces between the columns along the walkway, so that even those statues wearing Greek cloaks appear to be doing gardening and selling the ivy. Then there is the changing room, which is the coolest place and the most covered in moss.

There you have virtually all the news from country. That man Philotimus, together with Cincius, is pressing on with the finishing touches to your house in town, but I frequently go over and take a look myself, which is easy to do. So, I hope you're free from any concern about it.

12 THE DECORATOR MUST UNDERSTAND YOUR VISION

Essential to the decoration of an elegant Roman home was the procurement and display of statues, paintings, and mosaics. Cicero enlisted his friend Fabius Gallus to purchase art to ornament his country house. The first paragraphs of this letter from Cicero to Gallus reveal how the arrangement soured: Gallus acquired statues from Avianius at an inflated price, blowing through the allocated budget and leaving Cicero in Avianius's debt. What was worse, the statues represented Bacchantes (Maenads), female followers of the wine god Bacchus known for their frenzy and emotional abandon. In Cicero's view, such figures are hardly suitable to adorn domestic spaces tailored to scholarly contemplation; but he takes comfort in a certain Damasippus's assurance that he himself will buy any statue Cicero rejects.

The last part of the letter reveals that Gallus has purchased a house in Rome near to Cicero's own. Cicero discusses his and Gallus's efforts through proxies to encourage the former owner Cassius and his sister Licinia to vacate the premises in a timely fashion. Only then can they enjoy the friendly intimacy made possible by physical proximity. Cicero's dependence on the bargaining skills of his daughter Tullia in this episode offers a rare window into how restrictive gender norms paradoxically propelled Roman women into negotiations typically conducted by men: for Cicero to broach the matter with Licinia directly might endanger her *pudicitia* (reputation as a chaste woman).

This letter of December, 46 BCE, alongside others written to his friend Atticus, suggests that Cicero valued a coherent design aesthetic based on subject matter above all else. It is possible, however, that previous instructions or conversations about material, style, period, or artist may have informed Gallus's selections as well.

7.23

Cicero salutem dicit M. Fabio Gallo

Tantum quod ex Arpinati ueneram cum mihi a te
litterae redditae sunt ab eodemque accepi Auiani litteras, in quibus hoc inerat liberalissimum, nomina se
facturum cum uenisset qua ego uellem die. fac, quaeso,
qui ego sum esse te: estne aut tui pudoris aut nostri
primum rogare de die, deinde plus annua postulare?
sed essent, mi Galle, omnia facilia si et ea mercatus
esses quae ego desiderabam et ad eam summam quam
uolueram. ac tamen ista ipsa quae te emisse scribis
non solum rata mihi erunt sed etiam grata. plane enim
intellego te non modo studio sed etiam amore usum
quae te delectarint, hominem, ut ego semper iudi-
caui, in omni iudicio elegantissimum, quae me digna
putaris, coemisse. sed uelim maneat Damasippus in
sententia; prorsus enim ex istis emptionibus nullam
desidero. tu autem, ignarus instituti mei, quanti ego
genus omnino signorum omnium non aestimo tanti
ista quattuor aut quinque sumpsisti. Bacchas istas cum
Musis Metelli comparas. quid simile? primum ipsas
ego Musas numquam tanti putassem atque id fecissem
Musis omnibus approbantibus, sed tamen erat aptum
bibliothecae studiisque nostris congruens; Bacchis
uero ubi est apud me locus? at pulchellae sunt. noui
optime et saepe uidi. nominatim tibi signa mihi nota

Cicero, *Epistulae ad familiares*

Cicero sends his greetings to M. Fabius Gallus.

The moment I arrived from Arpinum, your letter was handed to me. Simultaneously, I received a letter from Avianius, with the very generous offer that he would loan me the balance owed. I am begging you, put yourself in my place. Doesn't it seem beneath my dignity, and yours, first to request credit, and then to drag it out a year? Really, it would all be so simple, dear Gallus, if you had just bought what I wanted within the limit I was willing to spend. Nevertheless, the items you write to say that you purchased will be approved and appreciated. I can clearly recognize that you acted not just with connoisseurship but with passion when acquiring pieces that interested you—I have always considered you eminently discerning—and that you thought suitable for me. I do hope, however, that Damasippus doesn't change his mind, since I have no interest in any of these. You, on the other hand, unacquainted as you are with my approach, have purchased four or five of these pieces for a price I would not have considered a bargain for all the statues in the world. You compare these Bacchantes of yours with Metellus's Muses. How are they alike? In the first place, I would never have priced the Muses themselves

mandassem si probassem. ea enim signa ego emere
soleo quae ad similitudinem gymnasiorum exornent
mihi in palaestra locum. Martis uero signum quo mihi
pacis auctori? gaudeo nullum Saturni signum fuisse;
haec enim duo signa putarem mihi aes alienum attu-
lisse. Mercuri mallem aliquod fuisset; felicius, puto,
cum Auianio transigere possemus.

Quod tibi destinaras trapezophorum, si te delectat,
habebis; sin autem sententiam mutasti, ego habe<b>o
scilicet. ista quidem summa ne ego multo libentius
emerim deuersorium Tarracinae, ne semper hospiti
molestus sim. omnino liberti mei uideo esse culpam,
cui plane res certas mandaram, itemque Iuni, quem
puto tibi notum esse, Auiani familiarem. exhedria
quaedam mihi noua sunt instituta in porticula Tuscu-
lani. ea uolebam tabellis ornare. etenim, si quid generis
istius modi me delectat, pictura delectat. sed tamen
si ista mihi sunt habenda, certiorem uelim me facias

so high, and they would all agree with me! Nevertheless, Muses would have been appropriate for a library and consistent with my interests. Where in my home, in all honesty, is there a setting for Bacchantes? "Oh, but they are adorable." Yes, I'm highly familiar with them; I've seen them everywhere. I would have asked you for statues I knew by name, if I had placed any value on them. I am used to buying the kind of statue that can make a spot in my Roman exercise ground beautiful, the way they do in the Greek variety.[1] What good is a statue of Mars to me, a champion of peace? I'm glad that there was no statue of Saturn; I'd hate to imagine those two statues controlling my debt.[2] I would rather there had been some representation of Mercury; in that case, we might be able to transact more favorably with Avianius.

If you like the table with sculpted legs that you chose, you can have it for yourself; but if you have changed your mind, I will take it, of course. For that high a price, I would be a lot happier purchasing a pied-à-terre at Tarracina,[3] so that I am not always such a nuisance to my host. I see that this is absolutely my freedman's fault—I sent him clear instructions—and Junius's too, I think you know him, Avianius's friend. I have had some new alcoves built onto the little colonnade at my home in Tusculum,[4] and I have been wanting to decorate them

ubi, sint, quando arcessantur, quo genere uecturae. si enim Damasippus in sententia non manebit, aliquem Pseudodamasippum uel cum iactura reperiemus.

Quod ad me de domo scribis iterum, iam id ego proficiscens mandaram meae Tulliae; ea enim ipsa hora acceperam tuas litteras. egeram etiam cum tuo Nicia, quod is utitur, ut scis, familiariter Cassio. ut redii autem, priusquam tuas legi has proximas litteras, quaesiui de mea Tullia quid egisset. per Liciniam se egisse dicebat (sed opinor Cassium uti non ita multum sorore); eam porro negare se audere, cum uir abesset (est enim profectus in Hispaniam Dexius), illo et absente et insciente migrare. est mihi gratissimum tanti a te aestimatam consuetudinem uitae uictusque nostri primum ut eam domum sumeres ut non modo prope me sed plane mecum habitare posses, deinde ut migrare tanto opere festines. sed ne uiuam si tibi concedo ut eius rei tu cupidior sis quam ego sum. itaque omnia experiar. uideo enim quid mea intersit, quid

with paintings. The fact is, if I could get excited about anything like that,[5] it would be a painting. Nevertheless, if I have to keep these items of yours, please let me know where they are, when they are being shipped, and how they are being transported. If Damasippus does change his mind, we will find some other Damasippus, even if it means I take a loss.

The second matter you wrote to me about is the house. As I was leaving, I gave instructions to my daughter Tullia, since I received your letter just then. I even contacted your friend Nicias, because he considers Cassius a close friend, as you know. When I got back, before I read your last letter, I asked my Tullia what progress she had made. She said that she had been handling things through Licinia (though I am not sure Cassius has all that much to do with his sister), and that Licinia, in turn, had said she would not dare, while her husband was away (Dexius has left for Spain), to move, while he was gone and without him knowing. It means a lot to me that you valued being a part of my everyday life so much that you bought a house where you could live not just next door to me, but really by my side, and also that you are in such a hurry to move into it. But I won't allow to you believe you are more eager for this arrangement than I am.

utriusque nostrum. si quid egero, faciam ut scias. tu
et ad omnia rescribes et quando te exspectem facies
me, si tibi uidetur, certiorem.

Therefore, I will make every effort. I can see how relevant this is to my interests, and really to both our interests. If I make any progress, I will let you know. Meanwhile, if you don't mind, keep me up to date on all of this and confirm when I should expect you.

13 SO YOUR ARCHITECT BLEW THROUGH THE BUDGET: NOW WHAT?

Architectural construction is high risk. We know little about the kinds of contracts that bound home-owners and architects or builders in Roman antiquity, including how much protection there was for either party. While state contracts are preserved from various sites around the Mediterranean basin, they do not survive in a quantity that offers scope to draw many conclusions about norms. A passage from Vitruvius's *De architectura* provides a window into public procurement and advances the idea that contractors should be held liable for overrunning project budgets.

The law of Ephesus that Vitruvius mentions may be fictional, as there is no evidence that such a legal requirement or norm ever existed there. Vitruvius, moreover, often uses ostensibly historical anecdotes, set in the Greek East, to advance his own suggestions as to how Roman architectural practices should change. Nevertheless, the very use of this anecdote to bolster his suggestion is telling: for an architectural author to focus his attentions on the real or imagined faults of practitioners reveals the lengths to which Vitruvius will go to assure the homeowners among his readers that he perfectly understands their frustrations and fears. The passage also suggests a timelessness to the psychology of price overruns: while overrunning the budget by a little is often stomachable, each person has a tipping point at which additional expenses can no longer be financially or emotionally sustained.

Nobili Graecorum et ampla ciuitate Ephesi lex uetusta dicitur a maioribus dura condicione sed iure esse non iniquo constituta. nam architectus, cum publicum opus curandum recipit, pollicetur quanto sumptu id sit futurum. tradita aestimatione magistratui bona eius obligantur, donec opus sit perfectum. absoluto autem, cum ad dictum inpensa respondit, decretis et honoribus ornatur. item si non amplius quam quarta ad aestimationem est adicienda, de publico praestatur, neque ulla poena tenetur. cum uero amplius quam quarta in opere consumitur, ex eius bonis ad perficiendum pecunia exigitur.

Utinam dii inmortales fecissent ea lex etiam P. R. non modo publicis sed etiam priuatis aedificiis esset constituta! namque non sine poena grassarentur inperiti, sed qui summa doctrinarum subtilitate essent prudentes, sine dubitatione profiterentur architecturam, neque patres familiarum inducerentur ad infinitas sumptuum profusiones et ut e bonis eicerentur, ipsique architecti poenae timore coacti diligentius modum inpensarum ratiocinantes explicarent, uti patres familiarum ad id quod praeparauissent, seu paulo amplius adicientes, aedificia expedirent. nam

Vitruvius, *De architectura*

In the prominent and vast Greek city of Ephesus, reputedly, a time-honored law was laid down by people living in a previous age, in harsh terms, but legally sound, to the effect that an architect, when he undertakes the construction of a public work, guarantees at what cost it will happen. After the estimate is handed over, his property is pledged to the magistrate as collateral, until the work is finished. Upon completion, when the cost corresponds to the agreement, he is rewarded by honorary decrees. If no more than a quarter must be added to the estimate, it is supplied by the state, and the architect is not penalized. But if more than that quarter is spent on the work, the money to finish the job is exacted from the architect's property.

If only the immortal gods had brought it about that this law had been enacted at Rome not only for public, but also for private buildings! In that case, unqualified people would not be prowling around with impunity, but instead those with a practical understanding of the science and the sharpest attention to detail would practice architecture without any hesitation, and also *patres familiarum*[1] would not be deluded into unlimited outpourings of investment, such that they are even dispossessed of their property, and the architects themselves, compelled by the fear of a

qui quadringenta ad opus possunt parare, si adicient
centum, habendo spem perfectionis delectationibus
tenentur; qui autem adiectione dimidia aut ampliore
sumptu onerantur, amissa spe et inpensa abiecta, fractis rebus et animis desistere coguntur.

penalty, when keeping their accounts would more carefully lay out the extent of the cost, so that *patres familiarum* would complete their constructions for the amount they had set aside for them, or by throwing in a little more. For those who are able to offer 400,000 [sesterces] for the work, if they have to throw in 100,000 more, are kept happy by possessing the expectation of its completion, while those who are burdened with an addition of a half or more of the expense, with hope abandoned and the sum wasted, their finances and peace of mind shattered, are compelled to give up.

14 WHEN REDECORATING, USE THE MOST EXPENSIVE MATERIALS THE LEAST

A highly distinctive feature of Roman décor was the use of bright colors to enliven walls with patterns, pictures, or simply in monochrome. *De architectura* 7, Vitruvius' volume on the finishing touches of architecture, details the sources, preparation, and application of paint pigments. Many of these colors, including vibrant greens, purples, and blues, were imported to Italy from afar and commanded high prices. The most expensive pigment used in Roman wall painting was vermilion, also referred to as cinnabar or, more casually, "Pompeian red," today. Vermilion is a bright, rich red that gleams and sparkles in the sun. Ironically, vermilion is vulnerable to irreversible darkening when unprotected from light exposure. Vitruvius obliquely signals the moral hazard that attaches to this opulently luxurious substance by telling the story of a scribe named Faberius. Roman scribes, as members of a rapidly expanding and upwardly mobile bureaucratic class, were frequently condemned as ambitious upstarts and pilloried for their extravagance. In this cautionary tale, Faberius' overzealous application of vermilion quickly becomes its own punishment.

Quod enim antiqui insumentes laborem et industriam probare contendebant artibus, id nunc coloribus et eorum eleganti specie consecuntur, et quam subtilitas artificis adiciebat operibus auctoritatem, nunc dominicus sumptus efficit ne desideretur.

Quis enim antiquorum non uti medicamento minio parce uidetur usus esse? at nunc passim plerumque toti parietes inducuntur. accedit huc chrysocolla, ostrum, armenium. haec uero cum inducuntur etsi non ab arte sunt posita, fulgentes oculorum reddunt uisus, et ideo quod pretiosa sunt, legibus excipiuntur ut a domino, non a redemptore repraesententur.

■ ■ ■

Itaque cum est in expolitionibus conclauium tectis inductum, permanet sine uitiis suo colore; apertis uero, id est peristyliis aut exhedris aut ceteris eiusdem modi locis, quo sol et luna possit splendores et radios immittere, cum ab his locus tangitur, uitiatur et amissa uirtute coloris denigratur. itaque cum et alii multi tum etiam Faberius scriba, cum in Auentino uoluisset

Vitruvius, *De architectura*

That which, unquestionably, the earlier generation, expending labor and diligence, strove to demonstrate through artistry, now is achieved through colors and their elegant appearance, and the authority buildings once gained by their fine craftsmanship now is not missed on account of what the patron's lavish expenditure accomplishes.

Who of the earlier generation does not seem to have used vermilion sparingly, as if they were taking medicine?[1] Added to this by patrons today are malachite green, purple, and Armenian ultramarine. When these colors are used, even if they are not applied with skill, they render a gleaming appearance, and because they are expensive, they are exempted from the contracts, so that they are paid for in cash by the homeowner and not by the contractor.

■ ■ ■

When vermilion is included in the finishing touches of fully enclosed spaces, it maintains its own color without defects; but in open places, such as peristyles and exedras and so forth, where the sun and the moon can send their gleaming shafts of light, the affected surface is damaged and becomes black, as the color loses its strength. Thus, when many

habere domum eleganter expolitam, peristyliis parietes omnes induxit minio, qui post dies XXX facti
sunt inuenusto uarioque colore. itaque primo locauit
inducendos alios colores.

others were doing the same thing, even Faberius the scribe, since he wanted to own an elegantly decorated house on the Aventine hill,[2] covered all his peristyle walls with vermilion, which after thirty days became distasteful and discolored. As a consequence, he immediately contracted for repainting with other colors.

15 OVERSPEND, AND YOUR HOME COULD RUIN YOU

Being book-wise doesn't mean that you're street-wise. Publius Valerius Cato (ca. 95–20s BCE) was an acclaimed teacher, specializing in literary subjects, of the Roman elite, as well as an accomplished poet in his own right. This poem mocks Cato for falling into debt and destitution, despite being one of the intellectual luminaries of his generation. Praise for Cato as being on par with Zenodotus and Crates—two earlier, acclaimed scholars associated with the famous libraries of Alexandria and Pergamon—may be tongue-in-cheek, given the levity implied by the hyperbolic image of Cato's impoverishment: the teacher who once had an estate in the rich suburban area of Tusculum now has only a pile of splinters and single roof tile to shelter him.

We are given to assume that Cato went into debt by indulging in conspicuous luxuries, such as the exorbitantly expensive vermilion paint that once coated his now ruinous walls. A statue of the fertility god Priapus was a common sight in Roman gardens, but here its presence serves to underscore the contrast between the life of pleasure that Cato has been forced to leave behind and his current subsistence on rough fare. A final irony is that Cato, with his implied intellectual pretensions, is now compelled by poverty to survive on the vegetarian diet endorsed by philosophers as an antidote to opulence.

The poem is addressed to a person named Gallus, who may be the soldier and poet Cornelius Gallus. Its author is the little-known Roman poet Bibaculus (first century BCE).

fragments 2 and 1

Catonis modo, Galle, Tusculanum
tota creditor urbe uenditabat.
mirati sumus unicum magistrum,
summum grammaticum, optimum poetam,
omnes soluere posse quaestiones,
unum deficere expedire nomen.

en cor Zenodoti, en iecur Cratetis!

■ ■ ■

si quis forte mei domum Catonis,
depictas minio assulas, et illos
custodis uidet hortulos Priapi,
miratur quibus ille disciplinis
tantam sit sapientiam assecutus,
quem tres cauliculi, selibra farris,
racemi duo tegula sub una
ad summam prope nutriant senectam.

Bibaculus

Gallus, only just now a creditor was peddling
Cato's Tusculan property all around town.
I was amazed that this peerless teacher,
this towering scholar, this supreme poet
could untangle every research problem
but failed to extricate his name once from a creditor's
    list.
Behold, the mind of Zenodotus! Behold, the soul of
    Crates!

■ ■ ■

If by chance anyone sees my friend Cato's house,
splinters decorated with vermilion paint, and sees that
little garden with Priapus standing guard,
he wonders from what areas of study
he has achieved such wisdom
that three cabbage sprouts, half a pound of wheat,
and two clusters of grapes can keep him fortified,
under a single roof tile, to the brink of old age?

16 NEGLECTED HOUSE, NEGLECTED SOUL

To preserve the structural integrity of a Roman home was a sacred duty; for that reason, a derelict house was a potent symbol of moral decline. In a comedy by the playwright Plautus (third to second century BCE), a drunken young man named Philolaches careens onstage with the intent to lecture the audience on some deep thoughts that have just occurred to him—if only he can steady himself long enough to string together the sequence of thought. Philolaches's idea is that people are like houses, in that it is not enough that they are designed, constructed, and embellished with care; they must also be properly maintained. This is a doubly painful truth for Philolaches to realize, as he is on a bender that will leave the family home and finances, not to mention his own character and reputation, in rough shape.

Recordatu' multum et diu cogitaui

argumentaque in pectus multa institui
ego, atque in meo corde, si est quod mihi cor,
eam rem uolutaui et diu disputaui,

    hominem quoiiu' rei, quando natus est

similem esse arbitrarer simulacrumque habere
    id repperi iam exemplum.[1]
nouarum aedium esse arbitro similem ego hominem
quando hic natus est. ei rei argumenta dicam.
atque hoc hau uidetur ueri simile uobis,
    at ego id faciam esse ita ut credatis.
profecto esse ita ut praedico uera uincam.

atque hoc uosmet ipsi, scio, proinde uti nunc

ego esse autumo, quando dicta audietis
    [mea], haud aliter id dicetis.
auscultate, argumenta dum dico ad hanc rem:
simul gnaruris uos uolo esse hanc rem mecum.

aedes quom extemplo sunt paratae, expolitae,
    factae probe examussim,

Plautus, *Mostellaria*

I've thought about this a lot and reflected on it at
    length.
In my mind, I have entertained endless debate,
and in my heart (if I even have one)
I have turned this thing around and examined it for a
    long time:
what should I consider a person to be similar to, what
    is the thing
most like a person, when a person is born?
I have now discovered this analogy.
I think a person, when first born,
is like a new house. I will supply my evidence of this.
To you, this won't even seem close to the truth,
but I'll make sure that you believe it.
Undoubtedly, I will convince you that all of this is just
    as I say.
And you yourselves, when you hear my words, I'm
    sure,
will say it is not otherwise
than how I now affirm that it is!
Listen while I produce my evidence for this idea.
I want you to know as much as I do about it.

As soon as a house is ready for moving in, completed
    with high-end finishes,
constructed with total precision,

laudant fabrum atque aedes probant, sibi quisque inde
　　　　　　　　　　　　　　　exemplum expetunt,
sibi quisque similis uolt suas, sumptum, operam <parum>
　　　　　　　　　　　　　　　　　parcunt suam.
　atque ubi illo immigrat nequam homo, indiligens

　cum pigra familia, inmundus, instrenuos,
hic iam aedibus uitium additur, bonae quom curantur male;
　atque illud saepe fit: tempestas uenit,

　confringit tegulas imbricesque: ibi
　dominus indiligens reddere alias neuolt;
　uenit imber, lauit parietes, perpluont,
　tigna putefacit, perdit operam fabri:
　nequior factus iam est usus aedium.

　atque <ea> haud est fabri culpa, sed magna pars

morem hunc induxerunt: si quid nummo sarciri potest,

　usque mantant neque id faciunt donicum
parietes ruont: aedificantur aedes totae denuo.

the owners compliment the builder and they approve
   of the house,
and everyone else seeks this house out as a model for
   their own.
Everybody wants their own houses to be similar,
and they don't spare any expense or even their own
   labor to make it so.
But when a good-for-nothing, lazy, unhygienic,
   negligent homeowner moves in
with a slovenly family, this now creates a defect in the
   house,
even though it's still a good house, just badly cared for.
And then, as so often happens, a storm comes
and breaks the roof tiles and gutter tiles, and
the careless owner does not want to replace them with
   others.
A rain shower comes on and streams down the walls;
   they leak;
it causes the beams to rot; it destroys the builder's
   accomplishments;
then the integrity of the house becomes compromised.
And, in fact, this is not the builder's fault. Instead, the
   majority of people
have adopted this habit: if anything costs money to be
   repaired,
they wait around and don't do it,
until the walls collapse, and the whole house has to be
   rebuilt.

haec argumenta ego aedificiis dixi; nunc etiam uolo

dicere uti homines aedium esse similis arbitremini.
primumdum parentes fabri liberum sunt:

i fundamentum supstruont liberorum;

extollunt, parant sedulo in firmitatem,

et ut <et> in usum boni et in speciem

poplo sint sibique, hau materiae reparcunt
nec sumptus ibi sumptui ducunt esse;

expoliunt: docent litteras, iura, leges,

sumptu suo et labore

nituntur ut alii sibi esse illorum similis expetant.

ad legionem quom ita * * * adminiclum is danunt

tum iam, aliquem cognatum suom.
eatenus abeunt a fabris. unum ubi emeritum est
stipendium,
igitur tum specimen cernitur quo eueniat aedificatio.

NEGLECTED HOUSE, NEGLECTED SOUL

I have stated these pieces of evidence about buildings;
    now I also want to
tell you how you are to suppose that people are like
    houses.
In the first place, parents are the builders of their
    children;
they lay the foundations beneath their children.
They raise them up; they diligently rear them to be
    strong,
so that they are in good shape, both in practice and in
    appearance,
for their own benefit and in the opinion of others.
    They aren't sparing at all with materials,
and they don't consider an expense in that direction to
    be an extravagance.
They decorate them with high-end finishes: they teach
    them literature, ordinances, laws,
supplying their own financing and labor.
They toil away so that others might wish for their own
    children to be like to them.
When the children have been equipped in this way,
    they send them to the army,
and at that time they assign them some relation of
    theirs as a protector.
That's it. They go away from the builders. When they
    have completed one term of service,
then a sample is available to view, showing how the
    building may turn out.

nam ego ad illud frugi usque et probus fui
in fabrorum potestate dum fui.
postea quom immigraui ingenium in meum,
perdidi operam fabrorum ilico oppido.

uenit ignauia, ea mi tempestas fuit,
mihi aduentu suo grandinem imbrem[que] attulit;
haec uerecundiam mi et uirtutis modum
deturbauit detexitque a med ilico;
postilla optigere eam neglegens fui.

continuo pro imbre amor aduenit in cor meum,

is usque in pectus permanauit, permadefecit cor meum.
nunc simul res, fides, fama, uirtus, decus
deseruerunt: ego sum in usu factus nimio nequior.
atque edepol ita haec tigna umiditate putent: non uideor
                                         mihi
sarcire posse aedis meas quin totae perpetuae ruant,
cum fundamento perierint nec quisquam esse auxilio
                                        queat.
cor dolet quom scio ut nunc sum atque ut fui,
quo neque industrior de iuuentute erat

                * * * * arte gymnastica:
disco, hastis, pila, cursu, armis, equo

uictitabam uolup,

Certainly, up to that time I was unfailingly frugal and
    honorable,
while I was in the power of the builders.
After that, when I relocated at my own inclination,

at once I entirely spoiled the labors of the builders.
Idleness came; that was my storm.
As soon as it arrived, it brought down hail and rain
    showers;
this idleness overthrew my modesty and the bounds of
    virtue,
and removed the roof from me immediately.
After that, I neglected to protect myself.
At once, passion like a torrent entered my heart;
it flowed down continuously into my chest, drenching
    my heart thoroughly.
Now property, credit, fame, virtue, and honor

have forsaken me simultaneously; by my habits, I have
    become much worse,
and by god so rotten are these rafters of mine with
    moisture, I don't think I can
possibly patch up my house to prevent it all from com-
    pletely falling down,
as the very foundation disappears, and no one can help
    at all.
My heart pains me, when I consider how I am now and
    how I once was,

parsimonia et duritia discipulinae alieis eram,
optumi quique expetebant a me doctrinam sibi.

nunc, postquam nihili sum, id uero meopte ingenio
repperi.

a person than whom, from childhood, no one was more
    physically active,
either with the discus, the javelin, the ball, racing,
    weapons, or horses.
At that time, I was living a pleasurable life,
while being instructive to others in my frugality and
    austerity;
the elite were begging me to train them.
Now that I have become nothing, I have figured this
    out, all through my own character.

17 THEY DON'T MAKE THEM LIKE THEY USED TO

The ideal home, like its owner, enshrined Roman virtues. A letter by Seneca the Younger (4 BCE– 65 CE), philosopher and advisor to the emperor Nero, recounts his trip—almost a pilgrimage— to the villa of Scipio Africanus at Liternum, just north of the Bay of Naples. Scipio Africanus (236–184/3 BCE), the famous general and war hero, retired to this rural estate after he lost political favor in 188 BCE. By reputation, Liternum was short on natural beauty, especially as compared to nearby resorts like Baiae, which comes under fire in the letter as a fount of hedonistic pleasures. It quickly becomes clear, however, that for Scipio, beauty was beside the point.

Scipio was, by all accounts, the first Roman to build a villa in Campania. At 250 years old, this rustic retreat was already historic by the time of Seneca's visit. Seneca contrasts Scipio's simplicity and modesty with the extravagance of current tastes. It is no accident that the description of this country estate, with its emphasis on the villa's capacity, enclosure, and fortifications, calls to mind a military camp: the house is a monument to the man. The letter as a whole, which is excerpted here, paints Scipio Africanus in a flattering light: the general is portrayed as a wise man (*sapiens*), who uses his exile from the city of Rome to develop wisdom in line with the tenets of Stoic philosophy.

Seneca's portrayal of Scipio's villa lingers on its bathing facilities. Bathing, whether at home or in a public setting, was for some Romans an almost daily activity. Private bath complexes, particularly those heated by furnaces, were nevertheless considered a luxury. The high cost of the imported stone and complex water features found in these baths aroused moral outrage. Stoic philosophers, including Seneca himself, endorsed the position that bathing in any facility should be limited in frequency, duration, and temperature. Thus, the austerity of Scipio's baths occasions high praise.

As was the case for Seneca's letter 55 (passage 7), this letter addresses a recipient named Lucilius, who has not been identified with any known historical figure by that name.

Vidi uillam extructam lapide quadrato, murum circumdatum siluae, turres quoque in propugnaculum
uillae utrimque subrectas, cisternam aedificiis ac
uiridibus subditam quae sufficere in usum uel exercitus posset, balneolum angustum, tenebricosum ex
consuetudine antiqua: non uidebatur maioribus nostris caldum nisi obscurum. magna ergo me uoluptas
subiit contemplantem mores Scipionis ac nostros: in
hoc angulo ille "Carthaginis horror," cui Roma debet
quod tantum semel capta est, abluebat corpus laboribus rusticis fessum. exercebat enim opere se terramque (ut mos fuit priscis) ipse subigebat. sub hoc ille
tecto tam sordido stetit, hoc illum pauimentum tam
uile sustinuit: at nunc quis est qui sic lauari sustineat?
pauper sibi uidetur ac sordidus nisi parietes magnis
et pretiosis orbibus refulserunt, nisi Alexandrina
marmora Numidicis crustis distincta sunt, nisi illis
undique operosa et in picturae modum uariata circumlitio praetexitur, nisi uitro absconditur camera,
nisi Thasius lapis, quondam rarum in aliquo spectaculum templo, piscinas nostras circumdedit, in quas
multa sudatione corpora exsaniata demittimus, nisi
aquam argentea epitonia fuderunt. et adhuc plebeias
fistulas loquor: quid cum ad balnea libertinorum peruenero? quantum statuarum, quantum columnarum
est nihil sustinentium sed in ornamentum positarum

Seneca, *Epistulae morales*

I have examined the villa, constructed of stone blocks,[1] the wall encircling a grove, and the towers that stand on either side of the villa, acting as bulwarks. The cistern, tucked below all the buildings and greenery, has the capacity even to supply an army. The cramped bath is cloaked in darkness, in the traditional manner: it didn't seem to our ancestors that there could be a hot bath, unless it was dimly lit. Consequently, a pleasant thought has occurred to me as I reflect upon Scipio's way of life and our own. In this sequestered spot, that man dubbed the "terror of Carthage," whom Rome has to thank for being captured only once,[2] used to cleanse a body exhausted by agricultural labor! For he used to occupy himself with strenuous activity (as was the custom in ages past), and he brought the land under cultivation with his own hands. He stood beneath this roof, which is so humble; this floor, which is so ordinary, bore his weight. But who is there now who could bear to bathe that way? A person considers himself poor and lowly unless his walls shine brightly with large and expensive discs of precious stone,[3] unless marble shipped from Alexandria is relieved by thin slabs of Numidian yellow, unless the multi-colored painting on the surface of these marbles was painstakingly done

impensae causa! quantum aquarum per gradus cum fragore labentium! eo deliciarum peruenimus ut nisi gemmas calcare nolimus.

In hoc balneo Scipionis minimae sunt rimae magis quam fenestrae muro lapideo exsectae, ut sine iniuria munimenti lumen admitterent; at nunc blattaria uocant balnea, si qua non ita aptata sunt ut totius diei solem fenestris amplissimis recipiant, nisi et lauantur simul et colorantur, nisi ex solio agros ac maria prospiciunt.

everywhere and looks just like a picture, unless the vaulted ceiling is covered in glass;[4] unless fine white marble from Thasos, once an unusual sight in any temple, lines our swimming pools, into which we plunge our bodies once dehydrated from profuse sweating; and unless silver taps dispense the water. Up until this point I have been speaking about the pipes of ordinary people; what should I say when broaching the topic of baths belonging to freed slaves?[5] How many statues there are, how many columns supporting nothing, and only placed there as decoration, for the sake of spending money! How much water cascades smoothly, from level to level, with a roar! We have reached the point of such self-indulgence that we refuse to tread on anything but precious stones.

In this bath that belonged to Scipio there are slits, really, more than windows, cut out of the stone wall, such that they admit light without detriment to the building defenses; but nowadays people call baths moth havens if they have not been configured so as to receive sun exposure all day long through massive windows, if people cannot wash themselves and get a tan at the same time, and if they cannot see the countryside and the sea before them, from the bathtub.

18 THE GOLDEN MEAN

Success in Roman domestic design and home decoration was predicated on finding the right balance between frugality and extravagance. One homeowner described as particularly skilled in walking this tightrope, without incurring criticism in either direction, was Titus Pomponius Atticus (110–32 BCE). Atticus was a member of the high-ranking equestrian class and a banker, as well as a scholar.

In a biography of Atticus by Cornelius Nepos (ca. 110–25 BCE), an admiring description of Atticus's house reinforces the portrayal of his behavior and actions as well balanced, and thus in tune with the Aristotelian notion of "the mean." The house itself is primarily imagined through abstract terms that convey moral judgment, without much architectural or decorative specificity. Certain details, however, stand out as particularly evocative of Atticus's character, including the restraint with which he avoided unnecessary home renovation, and the focus within his home on books and literary activities.

THE GOLDEN MEAN

Atticus's pursuit of "the mean" resulted not just in a blameless home, but in an evenhanded approach to all things: while living in a turbulent time of shifting alliances, he remained neutral. Unlike the isolated and self-serving Vatia, described in Seneca's letter 55 (passage 7), however, Atticus's abstention from politics did not come at the cost of personal connections and the social obligation they entail. Indeed, Atticus is most famous for his close ties to statesmen at the center of Roman political life, most notably Cicero, with whom he corresponded extensively.

Neque uero ille minus bonus pater familias habitus est quam ciuis. nam cum esset pecuniosus, nemo illo minus fuit emax, minus aedificator. neque tamen non in primis bene habitauit omnibusque optimis rebus usus est. nam domum habuit in colle Quirinali Tamphilianam, ab auunculo hereditate relictam, cuius amoenitas non aedificio, sed silua constabat: ipsum enim tectum antiquitus constitutum plus salis quam sumptus habebat: in quo nihil commutauit, nisi si quid uetustate coactus est. usus est familia, si utilitate iudicandum est, optima, si forma, uix mediocri. namque in ea erant pueri litteratissimi, anagnostae optimi et plurimi librarii, ut ne pedisequus quidem quisquam esset, qui non utrumque horum pulchre facere posset, pari modo artifices ceteri, quos cultus domesticus desiderat, adprime boni. neque tamen horum quemquam nisi domi natum domique factum habuit: quod est signum non solum continentiae, sed etiam diligentiae. nam et non intemperanter concupiscere, quod a plurimis uideas, continentis debet duci, et potius diligentia quam pretio parare non mediocris est industriae. elegans, non magnificus, splendidus, non sumptuosus: omnisque diligentia munditiam, non affluentiam affectabat. supellex modica, non multa, ut in neutram partem conspici posset. nec praeteribo, quamquam nonnullis leue uisum iri putem, cum

Cornelius Nepos, *Atticus*

He, moreover, was regarded as no less admirable a head of household than he was a citizen. For although he was wealthy, no one was less acquisitive, no one less of a builder. Nevertheless, he lived exceptionally well and had the best of everything. He had a home, formerly Tamphilus's, on the Quirinal hill, which had been left to him as an inheritance by his maternal uncle; the appeal of it consisted not in the building itself, but in the grounds, since the dwelling, erected long ago, had more character than splendor. He made no changes to it, except when compelled by its age. The performance of his household staff, if judged by effectiveness, was optimal, if by outward appearance, scarcely average. Among them there were highly educated slaves, first-rate readers and a great many copyists, such that there was not even a single footman who could not perform both tasks very well. Likewise, the other specialists required for household management were particularly good. All of them were born and raised in his house: this is an indication not only of his restraint, but also of his financial management. It should be considered the mark of a restrained person not to be extravagantly covetous, as you would expect from a lot of people, and, what is more, to mobilize through exertion rather than

in primis lautus esset eques Romanus et non parum
liberaliter domum suam omnium ordinum homines
inuitaret, non amplius quam terna milia peraeque in
singulos menses ex ephemeride eum expensum sumptui ferre solitum. atque hoc non auditum, sed cogni-
tum praedicamus: saepe enim propter familiaritatem
domesticis rebus interfuimus.

Nemo in conuiuio eius aliud acroama audiuit quam
anagnosten, quod nos quidem iucundissimum arbitra-
mur; neque umquam sine aliqua lectione apud eum ce-
natum est, ut non minus animo quam uentre conuiuae
delectarentur: namque eos uocabat, quorum mores a
suis non abhorrerent. cum tanta pecuniae facta esset
accessio, nihil de cotidiano cultu mutauit, nihil de
uitae consuetudine, tantaque usus est moderatione,
ut neque in sestertio uicies, quod a patre acceperat,
parum se splendide gesserit neque in sestertio centies
affluentius uixerit, quam instituerat, parique fastigio
steterit in utraque fortuna. nullos habuit hortos, nullam suburbanam aut maritimam sumptuosam uillam,

investment is a mark of sound financial management. He was tasteful, not pretentious; illustrious,
not extravagant: and all his financial management
aspired to refinement, not profusion. His household
furnishings were modest and small in number, such
that they could be cited neither for showiness nor
surplus. Nor will I neglect to mention, although I
suppose to some it may seem trivial, that though he
was a Roman equestrian of pristine character and
graciously invited people of every echelon to his
home, he used to record on the ledger not more
than 3,000 sesterces paid towards his expenses in a
single month.[1] I mention this not as hearsay, but as
a direct observation, since often, on account of our
closeness, I was involved in his home life.

None of his dinner guests heard any performance,
other than a slave reading aloud, which is quite delightful, I think; there was never a dinner party at
his place without some reading, so that diners could
experience pleasure in their minds, not just in their
stomachs. He used to invite people whose lifestyles
were compatible with his own. When he came into a
lot of money, he changed none of his daily routines
and nothing about his lifestyle, and he showed such
moderation that just as he did not treat himself too
shabbily on the 2 million sesterces he had inherited
from his father, he also did not live more affluently
on 10 million sesterces than he had at the start, and

neque in Italia, praeter Arretinum et Nomentanum, rusticum praedium, omnisque eius pecuniae reditus constabat in Epiroticis et urbanis possessionibus. ex quo cognosci potest usum eum pecuniae non magnitudine, sed ratione metiri solitum.

he maintained his social standing in either financial state. He had no pleasure gardens, no luxurious villa near Rome, or at the seaside, or elsewhere in Italy, beyond his country estates at Arezzo and Mentana. All of his financial revenue derived from properties in Epirus and Rome, from which one can tell that he was used to assessing the performance of an asset not by its magnitude but by its governing principle.

19 THE CONSUMMATE VILLA, THE PERFECT HOME

A lengthy stroll through a tranquil villa, the pinnacle of excellence, ends this volume. There, spaces are defined not by their sumptuous materials or elegant furnishings, but by their orientation to the landscape and the spectacular views they afford. Home, we learn, is a not just the place where we are most ourselves. It is where humankind reconciles itself to the natural world.

The villa in question belongs to the author of the letter, Pliny the Younger (61–ca.113 CE), who invites his friend Gallus to stay with him and enjoy the serenity of the countryside. This is the longest and most detailed account of a single home that survives from Roman literature. Located at Laurentum, on the west coast of Italy, south of Rome, the villa is presented as Pliny's primary winter residence outside that city. The letter has inspired — and defied — repeated attempts to translate the sequence of rooms and buildings that Pliny describes into a coherent architectural blueprint or model (fig. 2). Efforts to locate the villa on the coast of Italy have

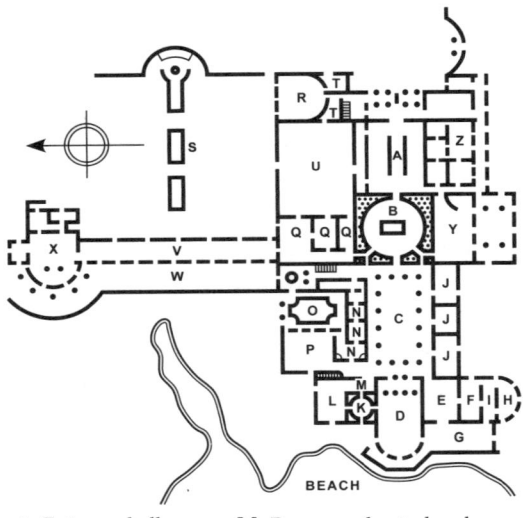

A. Entrance hall
B. Courtyard
C. Inner hall
D. Dining room
E. Bedroom
F. Bedroom
G. Gymnasium
H. Bedroom
I. Bedroom
J. Slaves' rooms
K. Bedroom
L. Small dining
   room
M. Rooms and antechambers
N. Bathrooms
O. Heated swimming bath
P. Ball court
Q. Suite with upper story
R. Dining room, stores above
S. Garden with vine pergola
T. Rooms behind dining room
U. Kitchen garden
V. Covered arcade
W. Terrace
X. Pliny's private suite
Y-Z. Kitchens and storerooms,
     not mentioned by Pliny

FIGURE 2. An imaginative reconstruction of the layout of Pliny's villa at Laurentum. Adapted from a drawing by Reginald Piggott, based on the model by Clifford Pember (1947).

likewise met with frustration. The natural conclusion to draw from this is that Pliny's Laurentian villa is best appreciated in the mind's eye, as an exquisite construction of words, rather than of bricks and mortar.

2.17

C. Plinius Gallo suo salutem

Miraris cur me Laurentinum uel (si ita mauis), Laurens meum tanto opere delectet; desines mirari, cum cognoueris gratiam uillae, opportunitatem loci, litoris spatium. decem septem milibus passuum ab urbe secessit, ut peractis quae agenda fuerint saluo iam et composito die possis ibi manere. aditur non una uia; nam et Laurentina et Ostiensis eodem ferunt, sed Laurentina a quarto decimo lapide, Ostiensis ab undecimo relinquenda est. utrimque excipit iter aliqua ex parte harenosum, iunctis paulo grauius et longius, equo breue et molle. uaria hinc atque inde facies; nam modo occurrentibus siluis uia coartatur, modo latissimis pratis diffunditur et patescit; multi greges ouium, multa ibi equorum boum armenta, quae montibus hieme depulsa herbis et tepore uerno nitescunt.

Pliny the Younger, *Epistulae*

Pliny sends his greetings to his dear Gallus.[1]

You may wonder why my Laurentine place (or my "Laurentian," if you prefer) entices me so much, but you will cease to wonder as soon as you become acquainted with the charm of the villa, the convenience of its location, and the extent of its shoreline. It is seventeen miles from Rome, so that once your business obligations are met, and the day has been safely put to bed, you can spend the night there. It can be reached by more than one route, since both the Via Laurentina and the Via Ostiensis lead in that direction, but you must get off the Via Laurentina at the fourteenth milestone from Rome and the Via Ostiensis at the eleventh. A side road splits off from both of these, which is sandy for a stretch; by carriage it is somewhat arduous and protracted, but it is quick and smooth on horseback. The view is varied from every direction, since at some stage the path is made narrower by woods blocking the way, and then it expands and opens out over far-reaching meadowlands where there are many flocks of sheep, many bands of horses and herds of cattle, which take on a healthy glow from the grass and the mild warmth of spring, once driven down from the mountains in winter.

Villa usibus capax, non sumptuosa tutela. cuius in prima parte atrium frugi, nec tamen sordidum; deinde porticus in D litterae similitudinem circumactae, quibus paruola sed festiua area includitur. egregium hae aduersus tempestates receptaculum; nam specularibus ac multo magis imminentibus tectis muniuntur. est contra medias cauaedium hilare, mox triclinium satis pulchrum, quod in litus excurrit ac si quando Africo mare impulsum est, fractis iam et nouissimis fluctibus leuiter adluitur. undique ualuas aut fenestras non minores ualuis habet atque ita a lateribus a fronte quasi tria maria prospectat; a tergo cauaedium porticum aream porticum rursus, mox atrium siluas et longinquos respicit montes.

Huius a laeua retractius paulo cubiculum est amplum, deinde aliud minus quod altera fenestra admittit orientem, occidentem altera retinet; hac et subiacens mare longius quidem sed securius intuetur. huius cubiculi et triclinii illius obiectu includitur angulus, qui purissimum solem continet et accendit. hoc hibernaculum, hoc etiam gymnasium meorum est; ibi omnes silent uenti, exceptis qui nubilum inducunt, et serenum

The house is spacious enough for my needs, but not expensive to maintain. At its entrance is an *atrium* that is modest, but not shabby, followed by colonnades curved in the shape of the letter D, in which a small but pretty courtyard is enclosed. These colonnades are an excellent refuge from storms, as they are fortified by windows and even more so by overhanging roofs. A bright *atrium* is in line with the center of the colonnades, then a quite attractive dining room, which projects outward towards the shore, and whenever the sea is driven back by the southwest wind, it is lightly lapped by the spray from the bursting white caps. All around, it has either folding doors or windows the size of doors, so that from the sides and front it affords views that create the impression of three seas, while at the rear it looks back through the *atrium*, a colonnade, the courtyard, the other colonnade, and next an *atrium* leading to the forest and the far-off mountains.

To the left of this, and set back slightly, is a large, private room, and then another, smaller one that lets in the rising sun through one window and holds onto the setting sun through the other; through the latter window, too, it has a remote but serene view of the sea lying beneath. At the junction of this private room and the aforementioned dining room is a secluded nook, which retains and intensifies the

ante quam usum loci eripiunt. adnectitur angulo cubiculum in hapsida curuatum, quod ambitum solis fenestris omnibus sequitur. parieti eius in bibliothecae speciem armarium insertum est, quod non legendos libros sed lectitandos capit. adhaeret dormitorium membrum transitu interiacente, qui suspensus et tubulatus conceptum uaporem salubri temperamento huc illuc digerit et ministrat. reliqua pars lateris huius seruorum libertorumque usibus detinetur, plerisque tam mundis, ut accipere hospites possint.

Ex alio latere cubiculum est politissimum; deinde uel cubiculum grande uel modica cenatio, quae plurimo sole, plurimo mari lucet; post hanc cubiculum cum procoetone, altitudine aestiuum, munimentis hibernum; est enim subductum omnibus uentis. Huic cubiculo aliud et procoeton communi pariete iunguntur.

direct sunlight. This is the winter quarters of my household staff, and also their exercise ground; there all the winds are still, except the ones that usher in rain clouds and banish clear skies, after which the place can be used again. Connected to the nook is a private room curved into an arc, which follows the course of the sun through each window. A bookcase is built into the wall of this room, in the semblance of a library, which holds books not just for reading but for reading over and over again. Adjoining this is a bedroom, separated by a passage, which, with a raised floor and piped walls, distributes and supplies captured air, calibrated to a healthy temperature, to the rooms on each side. The remaining part of this wing is reserved for the use of slaves and freed slaves, though most of the rooms are elegant enough that they could accommodate guests.

In the other wing is an extremely sophisticated private room, and then what can be used as either a large private room or a moderately sized dining room, which sparkles with the bounteous sun and the reflections off the sea; behind this is another private room with an antechamber, suited to summer on account of its high ceiling, but fully winterized by the reinforcement of its walls, as it is protected from every wind. Another private room similar to this one and an antechamber are joined by a shared wall.

inde balinei cella frigidaria spatiosa et effusa, cuius in contrariis parietibus duo baptisteria uelut eiecta sinuantur, abunde capacia si mare in proximo cogites. adiacet unctorium, hypocauston, adiacet propnigeon balinei, mox duae cellae magis elegantes quam sumptuosae; cohaeret calida piscina mirifica, ex qua natantes mare adspiciunt, nec procul sphaeristerium quod calidissimo soli inclinato iam die occurrit. Hic turris erigitur, sub qua diaetae duae, totidem in ipsa, praeterea cenatio quae latissimum mare longissimum litus uillas amoenissimas possidet. est et alia turris; in hac cubiculum, in quo sol nascitur conditurque; lata post apotheca et horreum, sub hoc triclinium, quod turbati maris non nisi fragorem et sonum patitur, eumque iam languidum ac desinentem; hortum et gestationem uidet, qua hortus includitur.

Gestatio buxo aut rore marino, ubi deficit buxus, ambitur; nam buxus, qua parte defenditur tectis, abunde uiret; aperto caelo apertoque uento et quamquam longinqua aspergine maris inarescit. adiacet gestationi interiore circumitu uinea tenera et um-

Beyond this are the expansive and sprawling cold rooms of the baths, in one room of which two plunge baths curve out sharply from opposite walls; they are of amply sufficient capacity, if you consider the proximity of the sea. Next come the massage room, the furnace room, and thereafter the sauna of the baths, and then two rooms more refined than luxurious, adjoined to the awe-inspiring, heated swimming pool, from which swimmers can gaze upon the sea.[2] Not far away is the ball court, which gets hit with the hottest sunshine, as soon as the day starts to slip away. Here a turret ascends, beneath which are two sets of rooms, the same as on the floor above, as well as a dining area, which commands a view of the outspread sea, a continuous shoreline, and the most charming houses. There is also another turret, in which there is a private room where the sun can be seen to rise and set, behind which is an extensive wine cellar and larder, and there is a dining room below, which is exposed only to the crashing sound of the turbulent sea, and even that is diminishingly faint; it looks onto the garden and the carriage path, which surrounds the garden.

The carriage path is outlined by a hedge of boxwood, or rosemary, where the boxwood fails, since boxwood, wherever it is shielded by buildings, will thrive abundantly; but when fully exposed to the sky and wind, it dries up on account of the salt spray,

brosa, nudisque etiam pedibus mollis et cedens. hortum morus et ficus frequens uestit, quarum arborum illa uel maxime ferax terra est, malignior ceteris. hac non deteriore quam maris facie cenatio remota a mari fruitur, cingitur diaetis duabus a tergo, quarum fenestris subiacet uestibulum uillae et hortus alius pinguis et rusticus.

Hinc cryptoporticus prope publici operis extenditur. utrimque fenestrae, a mari plures, ab horto singulae sed alternis pauciores. hae cum serenus dies et immotus, omnes, cum hinc uel inde uentis inquietus, qua uenti quiescunt sine iniuria patent. ante cryptoporticum xystus uiolis odoratus. teporem solis infusi repercussu cryptoporticus auget, quae ut tenet solem sic aquilonem inhibet summouetque, quantumque caloris ante tantum retro frigoris; similiter africum sistit, atque ita diuersissimos uentos alium alio latere frangit et finit. haec iucunditas eius hieme, maior aestate. nam ante meridiem xystum, post meridiem gestationis hortique proximam partem umbra sua temperat, quae, ut dies creuit decreuitue, modo breuior modo longior hac uel illa cadit. ipsa uero cryptoporticus tum maxime caret sole, cum arden-

even at a distance. A delicate vine trellis, affording plentiful shade, is adjacent to the carriage path on its inner circumference, and is soft and yielding to bare feet. Plentiful mulberry and fig trees blanket the garden; towards these types of trees, the soil is particularly conducive, though it is less hospitable to others. The dining room on the other side from the sea enjoys this view, which is no less desirable than that of the sea itself; it is surrounded in back by two suites of rooms, under the windows of which lies the entrance to the villa and another kitchen garden with rich soil.

From here, a covered arcade stretches out, almost as large as a public building. There are windows on every side, but there are more facing the sea, while facing the garden the windows are in an alternating pattern instead. These windows stay open without any issue—all of them when the day is cloudless and tranquil, and those on the side where the winds are quiet when the weather is turbulent on one side or another. In front of the covered arcade is a garden terrace fragrant with violets. It magnifies the warmth of the sun, enhanced by the reflection of the covered arcade, and this covered arcade obstructs and repels the cold northeast wind, just as it retains the sun, so that it is as hot in front as it is cool towards the back; in a similar manner, it blocks the southwest wind, and in this way curbs and curtails the winds from

tissimus culmini eius insistit. ad hoc patentibus fenestris fauonios accipit transmittitque nec umquam aere
pigro et manente ingrauescit.

In capite xysti, deinceps cryptoporticus horti, di-
aeta est amores mei, re uera amores: ipse posui. in hac
heliocaminus quidem alia xystum, alia mare, utraque
solem, cubiculum autem ualuis cryptoporticum, fenestra prospicit mare. contra parietem medium zoth-
eca perquam eleganter recedit, quae specularibus et
uelis obductis reductisue modo adicitur cubiculo
modo aufertur. lectum et duas cathedras capit; a pedibus mare, a tergo uillae, a capite siluae: tot facies loco-
rum totidem fenestris et distinguit et miscet. iunctum
est cubiculum noctis et somni. non illud uoces seruol-

different directions with its two sides; it is pleasant in winter, but even more so in summer, since before noon the covered arcade regulates the temperature of the garden terrace, and after noon it does the same for the closest part of the carriage path and garden with its shadow, which, as the day comes and goes, is cast first more narrowly, then at greater length on one side or the other. The covered arcade itself, of course, lacks sunlight the most when the sun lands with scorching directness on its roof. In addition to this, the arcade, with its wide-open windows, admits and circulates the western breezes and never becomes stagnant from still and sluggish air.

At the far end of the garden terrace, covered arcade, and garden is a suite that is really and truly my treasure: I commissioned it myself. Within it is a sunroom that faces the garden terrace on one side, the sea on the other, and the sun on both. Moreover, there is a private room with folding doors opening onto the covered arcade, and a window that provides a view of the sea. In the middle of the wall an alcove recedes extremely elegantly, which can be adjoined to or to shut off from the private room, according to whether the glass doors and curtains have been opened or closed. The alcove is roomy enough for a sofa and two easy chairs and has views of the sea beneath it, the villas at its back, and the woods to the fore: from its windows it offers up as many scenes

orum, non maris murmur, non tempestatum motus
non fulgurum lumen, ac ne diem quidem sentit, nisi
fenestris apertis.

Tam alti abditique secreti illa ratio, quod interi-
acens andron parietem cubiculi hortique distinguit
atque ita omnem sonum media inanitate consumit. ad-
plicitum est cubiculo hypocauston perexiguum, quod
angusta fenestra suppositum calorem, ut ratio exigit,
aut effundit aut retinet. procoeton inde et cubiculum
porrigitur in solem, quem orientem statim exceptum
ultra meridiem oblicum quidem sed tamen seruat.

In hanc ego diaetam cum me recepi, abesse mihi
etiam a uilla mea uideor, magnamque eius uoluptatem
praecipue Saturnalibus capio, cum reliqua pars tecti li-
centia dierum festisque clamoribus personat; nam nec
ipse meorum lusibus nec illi studiis meis obstrepunt.

of places individually as it does panoramas blending them into one. Next to it is a private room for use at night and for sleeping. Neither young slaves' voices, the roar of sea, the commotion of a storm, a flash of lightning, nor even daylight itself can penetrate this room, unless the shutters are open.

The explanation for such deep and withdrawn seclusion is that an intervening passageway separates the walls of this private room from those of the garden, and in so doing absorbs every sound with the emptiness that is in between. A small furnace chamber is linked to the private room, which either emits the heat from below, through a slit, or retains it, as the occasion requires. Then there is an antechamber and another private room, which faces out towards the sun, which it keeps hold of past noon, even if at an angle, having captured it the moment it rises.

Whenever I withdraw to this suite, I seem to have absented myself even from my own villa, and I take great pleasure from it, especially during the Saturnalia, when the rest of the building resounds with celebratory shouting and the liberties of the holiday, since I am not disrupting the amusement of my staff, nor they my concentration.

Haec utilitas haec amoenitas deficitur aqua sali-
enti, sed puteos ac potius fontes habet; sunt enim in
summo. et omnino litoris illius mira natura: quocum-
que loco moueris humum, obuius et paratus umor occurrit, isque sincerus ac ne leuiter quidem tanta maris
uicinitate corruptus. suggerunt adfatim ligna proxi-
mae siluae; ceteras copias Ostiensis colonia ministrat.
frugi quidem homini sufficit etiam uicus, quem una
uilla discernit. in hoc balinea meritoria tria, magna
commoditas, si forte balineum domi uel subitus adu-
entus uel breuior mora calfacere dissuadeat.

Litus ornant uarietate gratissima nunc continua nunc
intermissa tecta uillarum, quae praestant multarum
urbium faciem, siue mari siue ipso litore utare; quod
non numquam longa tranquillitas mollit, saepius frequens et contrarius fluctus indurat.

Mare non sane pretiosis piscibus abundat, soleas
tamen et squillas optimas egerit. uilla uero nostra

This accommodation, this pleasant spot, lacks only running water, but it has wells, or rather springs; they are very close to the surface. And altogether, there is a marvelous feature of that shore, in that wherever you disturb the soil, water, conspicuous and accessible, rushes to the surface, pure and not contaminated in the least by the sea's proximity. The forests nearby produce sufficient wood; the settlement of Ostia supplies the other provisions. But for a person of reasonable needs, a village, separated from mine by only one villa, has adequate resources. In this town, there are three public baths, a great advantage if by any chance a sudden arrival or a shorter stay discourages heating up the bath at home.

The structures of the villas, which are in some places clustered together, and in others spread apart, endow the sea shore with very pleasant variety, as they convey the impression of a number of cities, whether you take them in from the sea or from the shore itself, which an extended period of calm seas sometimes transforms into soft sand, but more often the repeated and punishing waves make firm.

The sea overflows with nearly worthless fish, but it does also yield sole and shrimp. My villa, on

etiam mediterraneas copias praestat, lac in primis;
nam illuc e pascuis pecora conueniunt, si quando
aquam umbramue sectantur.

Iustisne de causis iam tibi uideor incolere inhabi-
tare diligere secessum? quem tu nimis urbanus es nisi
concupiscis. atque utinam concupiscas! ut tot tantis-
que dotibus uillulae nostrae maxima commendatio ex
tuo contubernio accedat. uale.

the other hand, stands out for its excellent produce, even inland items, particularly milk; since farm animals converge on the villa from their pasturelands whenever they seek out water and shade.

Now do I seem to you justified in inhabiting, dwelling in, even loving my retreat? You're far too much of an urbanite if you don't covet it! And I hope you will covet it, so that the outstanding recommendation of your having stayed here may join the numerous and splendid attractions of my beloved villa. Farewell.

NOTES

Preface

1. For a survey of varying American responses to pandemic-induced work-from-home, see K. Parker, J. Menasce Horowitz, and R. Minkin, "COVID-19 Pandemic Continues to Reshape Work in America," Pew Research Center, February 16, 2022, available at https://www.pewresearch.org/social-trends/2022/02/16/covid-19-pandemic-continues-to-reshape-work-in-america/ (accessed October 30, 2024).

2. Statistics regarding vacillating house prices, including the Global House Price Index, are compiled by the International Monetary Fund.

3. A relevant communication from the European Commission is COM(2020)662: "Renovation Wave for Europe–Greening Our Buildings, Creating Jobs, Improving Lives" (limited version available at https://www.eumonitor.eu/9353000/1/j9vvik7m1c3gyxp/vlcxt8sqp3zo [accessed October 30, 2024]). Demand for architecture and design services in the United States is monitored by the American Institute of Architects. See, for example, the institution's press release of March 23, 2022: "Demand for Design Service

Continues to Grow," available at https://www.aiaiowa.org
/news/599979/Demand-for-design-service-continues-to
-grow.htm (accessed October 30, 2024).

4. One discussion of the phenomenon is I. Parker,
"HGTV is Getting a Renovation," *The New Yorker*, March
22, 2021.

Introduction

1. *De lingua latina* 8.16.31

2. *De lingua latina* 8.16.31: "uolumus [. . .] non domum
habere ut simus in tecto et tuto solum, quo necessitas con-
truserit, sed etiam ubi uoluptas retineri possit."

3. Glass window panes, available from the first century
CE, only became the norm centuries later.

4. *De architectura* 6.3.1–2. His fifth type, "testudinate,"
had no *compluuium* at all (i.e., the roof cover was unbroken).

5. *Satyrica* 29. This text, also known as the *Satyricon*,
probably dates to the second half of the first century CE.

6. In the translations to follow, the word *cubiculum* will
often be translated "bedroom."

7. *Satyrica* 77

8. *Satyrica* 77

9. *Epistulae* 4.6

10. *Res rustica* 2.1: "Viri magni nostri maiores non sine
causa praeponebant rusticos Romanos urbanis. ut ruri enim
qui in uilla uiuunt ignauiores, quam qui in agro uersantur in
aliquo opere faciendo, sic qui in oppido sederent, quam qui

rura colerent, desidiosiores putabant. [. . .] Quae nunc uix satis singula sunt, nec putant se habere uillam, si non multis uocabulis retinniat Graecis." See also *Res rustica* 3.2.3–4. The transliterated Greek word for exercise ground used here (*gymnasium*) underscores Varro's point.

11. *De architectura* 6.5.3

12. *Annales* 1.73

13. *De architectura* 6 and 7 can be easily accessed in Latin, with facing-page English translations, from the Loeb Library: F. Granger, ed. and trans., *Vitruvius: On Architecture*, vol. 2: *Books 6–10* (Loeb Classical Library 280) (Cambridge, MA: Harvard University Press, 1934).

14. One manifestation of these ideas was the worship of Vesta, goddess of the hearth fire, though paradoxically the ritual activities of her Vestal Virgins (the only major female priesthood at Rome) gave them a prominence in public life unlike that of other women.

1. Simplicity Is Bliss

1. The teller of this tale is the mythological hero Lelex, who hailed from Troezen in the northeastern Peloponnese in Greece. Pittheus was king of Troezen, but his father Pelops came from Phrygia (located in present-day central Turkey). Lelex does not elaborate further on why his ruler sent him to Phrygia.

2. The grandson of Atlas (and son of Jupiter) here described is Mercury. Mercury's staff (*caduceus*), entwined

with one or more snakes, shared its form with the wands carried by Greek and Roman heralds.

3. The referent of the adjective "pious" is ambiguous: it may refer to Baucis or to the home itself. (Punctuation, supplied by editors, was not a feature of the original Latin poem.)

4. A high staircase often led to the front entrance of a Roman temple.

5. Bithynia and Phrygia were neighboring lands in northwestern and western-central Anatolia (located in present-day Turkey).

2. How Houses Came to Be

1. The Colchians lived in present-day Georgia.

2. Marseille, the oldest city in France, was originally a Greek colony.

3. The city in question, as would be known to Vitruvius's early readers, is Rome.

3. Why Infrastructure Matters

1. *Antiquitates Romanae* 3.67.5

2. The politician Marcus Agrippa (ca. 63 BCE–12 BCE) assisted the emperor Augustus, often serving as his deputy.

4. Privacy is for Nobodies

1. See *De uiris illustribus* 66.1; Florus, *Epitome* 2.5–2.6

2. *Quaestiones Romanae* 81

5. A Home Should Reflect Its Owner

1. *Caua aedium* could be used interchangeably with *atrium*.

2. In accordance with Roman social norms, the less powerful conducted business by visiting the homes of their superiors, and not the other way around (see Introduction). For these room types, see fig. 1.

3. A basilica is a rectangular, roofed hall with interior space partitioned into aisles and a nave by columns or piers. Associations with Christianity (clearly) came later.

4. *De architectura* 1, as excerpted in the first passage of this section.

6. Don't Be Upstaged by Your House

1. Pliny the Elder, *Naturalis historia* 36.2.5–6. The capacity of the Theater of Marcellus must be roughly estimated, with the aid of written and archaeological sources.

2. This example is hardly chosen at random: Cicero was himself a "new man," without senators in his bloodline, and so his praise of a fellow aspiring politician from outside the hereditary ruling class betrays a self-interested motive.

3. Cicero here quotes a line of tragedy. Both the title of the play and the playwright are unknown.

4. Lucullus acquired fame (and infamy) for his extravagant private building projects that defied nature, even reversing the roles of land and sea by building over water. See Velleius Paterculus, *Historiae Romanae* 2.33.4.

7. Prime Real Estate Won't Solve
All Your Problems

1. A praetor was one of the highest-ranking magistrates in the Roman government.

2. This exclamation is ambiguous: in addition to "only you know how to stay alive," it could also mean "only you know how to live," or "you know how to live alone."

3. Or perhaps, "A wise person knows how to live alone, for himself."

4. The word translated as "trench" here, *euripus*, which is borrowed from Greek, can refer to a channel in the sea or other waterway, or to a trench dug between the arena and the seats of the Circus Maximus.

8. Displaying Portraits of Your Ancestors
Could Make You Look Shabby

1. The elite male addressee of the poem, Ponticus, has not been identified with a known historical figure.

2. The eight proper names associated with the Roman hereditary aristocracy (Aemiliani, Curii, Corvinus, Galba, Lepidi, Numantini, Fabius, and Allobrogici) in the first fourteen lines of the satire establish its ironic tone: a poem proposing that the importance of such names should be diminished nevertheless exhibits them front and center.

3. A censor was a high-ranking magistrate appointed to take the census (register citizens and their property), among other duties. A *magister equitum* was second-in-command

to a dictator. Dictators were appointed with complete and absolute power, on a temporary basis, in times of crisis. The title did not carry the negative connotations of autocratic rule by force that it does today.

4. Effeminate vanity, as illustrated by depilation, joins a series of moral failings (gambling, lust, untrustworthiness, cowardice). The Roman characterization of their ancestors as hirsute was a shorthand for praising their simplicity and unpretentiousness.

9. Unless You Have Deep Pockets, the Big City Is a Deathtrap

1. Prochyta was a tiny, barren island in the Bay of Naples, whereas the Subura was a gritty neighborhood in Rome.

2. During the sweltering (and malarial) month of August, being left behind in Rome as the more fortunate decamped to villas does not reflect well on these poets' reputation for quality verse.

3. Towns on the Italian peninsula in Etruria (located to the north of Rome) and Latium (the region in central Italy that included Rome).

4. While higher (or even penthouse) floors are often coveted in apartment buildings today, the reverse was true in Rome, where the ground floor was the safest and most commodious.

5. Cordus and Procula are characters otherwise unknown, but the context suggests that Procula's name evoked small stature.

6. Three towns in Latium.

7. Pythagoreans, followers of the Greek philosopher Pythagorus (sixth century BCE), were known to be vegetarian.

10. Caveat Emptor

1. If this Gaius Canius is the same as one known from other sources, this anecdote would appear to date to around the time of Cicero's birth (last quarter of the second century BCE).

2. The Latin word used here is *eques*, a member of the equestrian order, a property-based social class directly below the senatorial, or highest, class.

3. Pythius, whose name is Greek, is a figure otherwise unknown.

4. Gaius Aquilius Gallus, a Roman lawyer and statesman who lived in the mid-first century BCE, crafted the legal formula through which a person who had suffered loss through an act of bad faith could sue the person responsible.

5. The augurs were priests and the official Roman diviners. Augury was a religious practice through which observers interpreted the will of Jupiter as expressed by the behaviors of birds.

6. Centumalus is otherwise unknown, but Lanarius is attested for committing a political murder during the Sertorian War (80–72 BCE) which pitted Sulla and the Roman government against a group of rebels led by Sertorius.

7. The Cato who gave the verdict is Marcus Porcius Cato, tribune of the plebs in 99 BCE. His son Marcus Porcius

Cato (95–46 BCE), whom Cicero describes as the one "we know," was a proponent of Stoicism who famously committed suicide rather than submit to Julius Caesar during the Civil War. Father and son were descended, as grandson and great-grandson respectively, from the Marcus Porcius Cato (234–149 BCE), referred to as Cato the Elder (or Cato the Censor).

11. New Construction Requires Your Presence and Input

1. Arpinum, south of Rome in the region of Latium, was Cicero's birthplace.

2. Philotimus seems to have been a political functionary. Mescidium was a contractor, and Philoxenus may have been his assistant. Based on context, we may assume that Herus was Quintus's property manager, and enslaved.

3. This property seems to have been near Arcanum and known by the name of its previous owner (Manilius).

4. The Latin literally states that the Diphilus was "slower than Diphilus," an insult that makes the man's name a by-word for torpor.

12. The Decorator Must Understand Your Vision

1. The words for exercise ground that Cicero uses here, *palaestra* (Roman) and *gymnasium* (Greek), refer to large open courtyards often surrounded by colonnades. By Cicero's day, such facilities, used for exercise and intellectual pursuits, could be found in luxurious private homes as well.

2. Saturn (who devoured his own children) and Mars (god of war) are two particularly destructive Roman divinities, associated with bad luck in ancient astrology. On the other hand, Mercury, god of commerce, might bring Cicero good fortune.

3. Tarracina was located on the coast of Latium, midway between Rome and the Bay of Naples.

4. Tusculum, in Latium, was an area renowned for luxury villas.

5. The letter does not specify what the similarity is (subject? style?) between Gallus's previous purchases and the paintings Cicero might like.

13. So Your Architect Blew Through the Budget: Now What?

1. A plural form of *paterfamilias*, the head of a household.

14. When Redecorating, Use the Most Expensive Materials the Least

1. Vermilion had medicinal uses in antiquity, but in larger quantities, it was a poison.

2. Rome's Aventine hill was the site of an up-and-coming neighborhood at the time.

16 Neglected House, Neglected Soul

1. The quickly shifting meters of Philolaches' canticum give the typography of these lines a scattered appearance.

17. They Don't Make Them Like They Used To

1. Seneca here refers to *opus quadratum*, which we call ashlar masonry. The technique uses cuboid stones of the same size and shape in courses of "headers" (short end facing out) and "stretchers" (long end facing out) to present a smooth and even surface.

2. Rome was captured by the Gauls in 390 BCE (see Livy, *Ab urbe condita* 5.43–50)—but never, thanks to Scipio, by Hannibal.

3. The Latin word interpreted here to mean discs of precious stone (*orbibus*), may instead refer to mirrored surfaces.

4. This must refer to glass mosaics, which could adorn the surfaces of vaults.

5. In keeping with Roman class snobbery towards the previously enslaved, Seneca takes a dig at the conspicuous consumption of freed slaves.

18. The Golden Mean

1. This figure seems very low, even for such a moderate man; the explanation may be that Atticus's properties were largely self-sufficient.

19. The Consummate Villa, the Perfect Home

1. This Gallus may perhaps be identified with men of the same name mentioned or addressed in other letters written by Pliny; he has not been securely identified with a known historical figure.

2. Seneca laments the preference for such pools in letter 86 (passage 17).

PASSAGES TRANSLATED

1. Ovid, *Metamorphoses* 8.620–720

Tarrant, R. J., ed. *Ovid: Metamorphoses.* Oxford: Oxford University Press, 1981.

2. Vitruvius, *De architectura* 2.1.1–7

Callebat, L., ed. and trans. *Vitruve: De l'architecture II*, with introduction and commentary by P. Gros. Paris: Les Belles Lettres, 2003.

3. Strabo, *Geographica* 5.3.7–8

Sbordone, F., ed. *Strabonis Geographica*, vol. 2: *Libri III–VI*. Rome: Istituto Poligrafico dello Stato, 1970.

4. Velleius Paterculus, *Historiae Romanae* 2.13–14

Hellegouarc'h, J., ed., comm., and trans. *Velleius Paterculus: Histoire Romaine*, vol. 2: *Livre II*. Paris: Les Belles Lettres, 2003.

5. Vitruvius, *De architectura* 1.2.9 and Vitruvius, *De architectura* 6.5.1–3

Fleury, P., ed., comm., and trans. *Vitruve: De l'architecture I*. Paris: Les Belles Lettres, 2003.

Callebat, L., ed., comm., and trans. *Vitruve: De l'architecture VI*. Paris: Les Belles Lettres, 2004.

6. Cicero, *De officiis* 1.138–40

Winterbottom, M., ed. *M. Tulli Ciceronis: De officiis*. Oxford: Oxford University Press, 1994.

7. Seneca, *Epistulae morales* 55.3–8

Reynolds, L. D., ed. *L. Annaei Senecae: Ad Lucilium epistulae morales*, vol. 1: *Libri I–XIII*. Oxford: Oxford University Press, 1965.

8. Juvenal, *Saturae* 8.1–20

Clausen, W. V., ed. *A. Persi Flacci et D. Iuni Iuvenalis: Saturae*. Oxford: Oxford University Press, 1992.

I have departed from Clausen's text by printing *censorem* rather than *Coruinum* in line 7.

9. Juvenal, *Saturae* 3.1–9, 190–229, 268–77

Clausen, W. V., ed. *A. Persi Flacci et D. Iuni Iuvenalis: Saturae*. Oxford: Oxford University Press, 1992.

10. Cicero, *De officiis* 3.54–55, 58–61, 66–67

Winterbottom, M., ed. *M. Tulli Ciceronis: De officiis*. Oxford: Oxford University Press, 1994.

PASSAGES TRANSLATED

11. Cicero, *Ad Quintum fratrem* 3.1.1–2, 5–7

Shackleton Bailey, D. R., ed. and comm. *Cicero: Epistulae ad Quintum Fratrem et M. Brutum*. Cambridge: Cambridge University Press, 1980.

12. Cicero, *Epistulae ad familiares* 7.23

Shackleton Bailey, D. R., ed. and comm. *Cicero: Epistulae ad familiares*, vol. 2: *47–43 BC*. Cambridge: Cambridge University Press, 1997.

13. Vitruvius, *De architectura* 10, preface 1–2

Callebat, L., ed. and trans., with commentary by L. Callebat and P. Fleury. *Vitruve: De l'architecture X*. Paris: Les Belles Lettres, 2003.

14. Vitruvius, *De architectura* 7.5.7–8 and Vitruvius, *De architectura* 7.9.2

Liou, B. and M. Zuinghedau, eds and trans., with commentary by M.-T. Cam. *Vitruve: De l'architecture VII*. Paris: Les Belles Lettres, 2003.

15. Bibaculus, fragments 2 and 1

Kaster, R. A., ed., trans., and comm *C. Suetonius Tranquillus: De grammaticis et rhetoribus*. Oxford: Oxford University Press, 1995.

PASSAGES TRANSLATED

16. Plautus, *Mostellaria* 84–156

Lindsay, W. M., ed. *T. Macci Plauti: Comoediae*, vol. 2: *Miles gloriosus*; *Fragmenta*. Oxford: Oxford University Press, 2004 (repr.) [1905].

17. Seneca, *Epistulae morales* 86.4–8

Reynolds, L. D., ed. *L. Annaei Senecae: Ad Lucilium epistulae morales*, vol. 1: *Libri I–XIII*. Oxford: Oxford University Press, 1965.

18. Cornelius Nepos, *Atticus* 13–14

Marshall, P. K., ed. *Cornelii Nepotis: Vitae cum fragmentis*. Leipzig: Teubner, 1997.

19. Pliny the Younger, *Epistulae* 2.17

Mynors, R. A. B., ed. *C. Plini Caecili Secundi: Epistularum libri decem*. Oxford: Oxford University Press, 2013 (repr.) [1963].

My approach to numerous ambiguities in *Epistulae* 2.17 relies on Christopher Whitton's indispensable commentary:

Whitton, C., ed. *Pliny the Younger: Epistles, Book II*. Cambridge: Cambridge University Press, 2013.

FURTHER READING

On Townhouses

Clarke, J. R. *The Houses of Roman Italy, 100 BC–AD 250: Ritual, Space, and Decoration*. Berkeley, CA: University of California Press, 1991.

Leach, E. W. "*De exemplo meo ipse aedificato*: An Organizing Idea in the *Mostellaria*." *Hermes* 97, no. 3 (1969): 318–32.

Wallace-Hadrill, A. "The Development of the Campanian House," in J. J. Dobbins and P. W. Foss, eds, *The World of Pompeii*, 279–91. London: Routledge, 2007.

Wallace-Hadrill, A. *Houses and Society in Pompeii and Herculaneum*. Princeton, NJ: Princeton University Press: 1994.

On Villas

Becker, A. and N. Terrenato, eds. *Roman Republican Villas: Architecture, Context, and Ideology* (Papers and Monographs of the American Academy in Rome 32). Ann Arbor, MI: University of Michigan Press, 2012.

Bodel, J. "Monumental Villas and Villa Monuments." *Journal of Roman Archaeology* 10 (1997): 5–35.

Frazer, A., ed. *The Roman Villa: Villa Urbana*. Philadelphia: The University Museum, University of Pennsylvania, 1998.

Marzano, A. and G.P.R. Métraux, eds. *The Roman Villa in the Mediterranean Basin: Late Republic to Late Antiquity*. Cambridge: Cambridge University Press, 2018.

Mattusch, C. C., ed. *Pompeii and the Roman Villa: Art and Culture Around the Bay of Naples*. London: Thames & Hudson, 2008.

Purcell, N. "The Roman Villa and the Landscape of Production," in T. J. Cornell and K. Lomas, eds, *Urban Society in Roman Italy*, 151–79. London: Routledge, 1995.

Zarmakoupi, M. *Designing for Luxury on the Bay of Naples (c. 100 BCE–79 CE): Villas and Landscapes*. Oxford: Oxford University Press, 2014.

Zarmakoupi, M. *Shaping Roman Landscape: Ecocritical Approaches to Architecture and Wall Painting in Early Imperial Italy*. Los Angeles: Getty Publications, 2023.

On Domestic Space and the Identities of Those Who Lived and Worked There

Edwards, C. "Structures of Immorality: Rhetoric, Building, and Social Hierarchy," in Edwards, *The Politics of Immorality in Ancient Rome*, 137–72. Cambridge: Cambridge University Press, 1993.

Hackworth Petersen, L. *The Freedman in Roman Art and Art History*, esp. 123–83. Cambridge: Cambridge University Press, 2006.

Hales, S. *The Roman House and Social Identity*. Cambridge: Cambridge University Press, 2003.

Joshel, S. R. and L. Hackworth Petersen. "Slaves in the House," in Joshel and Hackworth Petersen, *The Material Life of Roman Slaves*, 24–86. Cambridge: Cambridge University Press, 2014.

Milnor, K. *Gender, Domesticity and the Age of Augustus: Inventing Private Life*. Oxford: Oxford University Press, 2005.

Nichols, M. F. *Author and Audience in Vitruvius' 'De architectura'*. Cambridge: Cambridge University Press, 2017.

On Decorating Homes with Art

Beacham, R. and H. Denard. *Living Theatre in the Ancient Roman House: Theatricalism in the Domestic Sphere*. Cambridge: Cambridge University Press, 2023.

Bergmann, B. "The Roman House as Memory Theater: The House of the Tragic Poet in Pompeii." *Art Bulletin* 76, no. 2 (1994): 225–56.

Elsner, J. "Viewing and Society: Images, the View and the Roman House," in Elsner, *Art and the Roman Viewer: The Transformation of Art from the Pagan World to Christianity*, 49–87. Cambridge: Cambridge University Press, 1995.

Gazda, E. K., ed. *Roman Art in the Private Sphere: New Perspectives on the Architecture and Decor of the Domus, Villa and Insula*. 2nd edn. Ann Arbor, MI: University of Michigan Press, 2010.

Jones, N. *Painting, Ethics, and Aesthetics in Rome*. Cambridge: Cambridge University Press, 2019.

Powers, J., ed. *Roman Landscapes: Visions of Nature and Myth from Rome and Pompeii*. San Antonio, TX: San Antonio Museum of Art, 2023.

Swift, E. *Style and Function in Roman Decoration: Living with Objects and Interiors*. Burlington, VT: Ashgate, 2009.

Valladares, H. *Painting, Poetry, and the Invention of Tenderness in the Early Roman Empire*. Cambridge: Cambridge University Press, 2021.

On Wall Paintings in the Home

Leach, E. *The Social Life of Painting in Ancient Rome and on the Bay of Naples*. Cambridge: Cambridge University Press, 2004.

Ling, R. *Roman Painting*. Cambridge: Cambridge University Press, 1991.

Mazzoleni, D., U. Pappalardo, and L. Romano. *Domus: Wall painting in the Roman House*. Los Angeles: J. Paul Getty Museum, 2004.

Pollitt, J. J., ed. *The Cambridge History of Painting in the Classical World*. Cambridge: Cambridge University Press, 2015.

Spina, L. *Inside Pompeii*. Los Angeles: Getty Publications, 2023.

FURTHER READING

On Mosaics in the Home

Dunbabin, K. *Mosaics of the Greek and Roman World*. Cambridge: Cambridge University Press, 2001.

Kondoleon, C. *Domestic and Divine: Roman Mosaics in the House of Dionysos*. Ithaca, NY: Cornell University Press, 1995.

On Construction and Architects

Anderson, J. C., Jr. *Roman Architecture and Society*. Baltimore: Johns Hopkins University Press, 1997.

Taylor, R. *Roman Builders: A Study in Architectural Process*. Cambridge: Cambridge University Press, 2003.